Powerful Poetry

Read, Write, Rejoice, Recite Poetry All Year Long

ADRIENNE GEAR

Pembroke Publishers Limited

To my late dad, who gifted me with his passion for poetry and his love of language. I know he would be happy to know I am passing it along.

© **2021 Pembroke Publishers**
538 Hood Road
Markham, Ontario, Canada L3R 3K9
www.pembrokepublishers.com

Funded by the Government of Canada
Financé par le gouvernement du Canada | Canada | ONTARIO CREATES

Library and Archives Canada Cataloguing in Publication

Title: Powerful poetry : read, write, rejoice recite poetry all year long / Adrienne Gear.

Names: Gear, Adrienne, author.

Identifiers: Canadiana (print) 20210277726 | Canadiana (ebook) 20210277823 | ISBN 9781551383521 (softcover) | ISBN 9781551389530 (PDF)

Subjects: LCSH: Poetry—Study and teaching. | LCSH: Poetics—Study and teaching.

Classification: LCC PN1101 .G43 2021 | DDC 808.1071—dc23

Editor: Kat Mototsune
Cover Design: John Zehethofer
Typesetting: Jay Tee Graphics Ltd.

Printed and bound in Canada
9 8 7 6 5

Contents

Preface

When I sent the manuscript draft of my most recent book, *Powerful Writing Structures,* to my editor in the fall of 2019, there was a sense of excitement mixed in with my relief. Relief, of course, that my manuscript was now in her capable hands, but excitement that I had managed to finally include poetry lessons in one of my books. For years, I had been wanting to write a book about teaching poetry, but my publisher had always felt that it was not a high priority and there might not be a large enough audience for it. With all the buzz about inquiry, critical and creative thinking, competencies alongside content, and educational equity, "how to write a haiku" did not appear high on the list of must-have educational resources. Including poetry lessons in my new writing book felt like a win for me. Poetry power, at last!

A few weeks later, I received an email from my editor: my book was too long and some cuts needed to be made. I almost knew it was coming before I got to the part when she explained that the easiest way to reduce the number of pages was to cut the poetry section completely. On a practical level, I knew she was right. But on an emotional level, I was gutted. Once again, there was no room for poetry.

My publisher, knowing how disappointed I was, suggested that I take the deleted lessons and write a supplementary book on poetry. But I had just finished writing a book and the thought of writing another one at that moment did not spark joy for me. Soon after my *Powerful Writing Structures* book was released, COVID-19 hit, and suddenly I found myself, like so many others, adjusting to some major life pivots. Writing a new book was simply not part of my pivot, so I sulked and filed away the deleted poetry lessons.

But they say things happen for a reason. Fast forward almost a year to January 26, 2021. On that day, then-unknown Amanda Gorman stood at the podium at incoming US President Joe Biden's inauguration and did more to put poetry on the map in ten minutes than the Romantics did in 300 years. There are not many moments when the masses get to experience poetry on such a grand scale and when they do, it makes a mark. (The only other time I can remember being moved by a poetry performance was when Canadian poet Shane Koyczan introduced the world to spoken-word poetry when he delivered "We Are More" at the opening ceremonies of the 2010 Winter Olympic Games in Vancouver.) The world watched Amanda, jaws dropped, hearts opened, as people witnessed and experienced an explosion of words, insight, strength, and power. As early as the next day, teachers were posting poetry lessons in response to Amanda's extraordinary poem. Social media lit up with Amanda Gorman memes and teens TikTok danced to the remix of "The Hill We Climb." Poetry was suddenly trendy. Immediately after Gorman's performance, I got a text from my dear friend Cheryl, who knew I would be watching. The text had only two words: *GET WRITING!* I may not be psychic, but somehow Amanda's poetry performance felt like a sign to me. And Cheryl was right. It was time to get writing.

Long before there was inquiry or competencies or student-based learning, there was poetry. It's been around for thousands of years and, while it may not be on every elementary teacher's radar, let me tell you this: it should be. Poetry promotes literacy, builds community, nudges our senses, and pulls at our emotions. In its entirety, poetry is an experience of sight, sound, emotion, and thought. Poetry has rhythm and beat and beauty all wrapped up in a flurry of words and phrases and white spaces. It fills our bodies, our ears, our souls, and helps us see the world with fresh eyes and an open heart. Poetry is powerful.

Jeanette Winterson says this about poetry: "*It isn't a hiding place. It's a finding place.*" In case you haven't figured it out by now, I found poetry a long time ago. But now I want to help you find it, too. And then, in turn, you can help your students find it. Poetry is everywhere—you just have to know where to look. So this book is my way of helping you and your students discover the "finding place" of poetry. Enjoy!

Introduction

"Teaching kids of all ages to write poetry, and to love to write and read poetry is probably my favorite teaching. It's sheer fun. It's exhilarating. Every child is successful. Each year, I am amazed at what kids can do, how insightful and clever they are, and what powerful poems they write." — Regie Routman

Teachers either love teaching poetry or they don't; they either avoid it and "run out of time" or make poetry a staple throughout their school year. For me, poetry is reading, writing, speaking, and celebrating language and, like Regie Routman, it's my favorite thing to teach. There is no better way to teach structure, language, and writer's craft than through poetry. There is no better way to bring joy into your classroom than to fill it with the sounds of poetry.

I was fortunate enough to grow up in a house filled with poetry. My father, a high-school English teacher, was passionate about it. More than anything, he loved words. He loved all things Shakespeare, Burns, Whitman, Keats, and Blake. Every Robbie Burns Day, after piping in the haggis, he stood at the dinner table and recited Robbie Burns poems to us. Even though he had spoken the same words by his beloved Scottish poet many times, my dad would often be moved to tears.

My late father gifted me with this love of language and passion for poetry. I started collecting quotes, words, and poems as a teenager and over the years recorded them in various Adrienne's Quote Collection notebooks. Despite strong advice against it by my good friend Cheryl, I even wrote poems to boyfriends in university. I have been referred to by friends and colleagues as a Quote Queen. I was a first-year teacher in the late 1980s when I sat down in a seat at the Dunbar Theatre in Vancouver one evening with Cheryl to watch the movie *Dead Poets Society*, starring Robin Williams. That movie, about an English teacher in a private boys' school, transformed me like no other. I have watched it dozens of times since. The character John Keating was the teacher who invited every student to stand on their desk because he wanted them to see the world differently; the teacher who played classical music at football practice and had players shout poetry before kicking the ball; the teacher who made a class of adolescent boys grow to love poetry and literature because he made it come alive for them. The teacher I wanted to be.

As a classroom teacher, I always loved teaching poetry to my students. Rather than teach a traditional poetry unit, I tended to sprinkle poetry throughout the year. When I became a literacy mentor with the Vancouver School Board and later a literacy support teacher at J.W. Sexsmith Elementary, I was always thrilled when a teacher would ask me to help them plan and teach a poetry unit. In my many years of working with them, there aren't many teachers I met who share my

"A poet is, before anything else, a person passionately in love with language." — W.H. Auden

"We don't read and write poetry because it's cute. We read and write poetry because we are members of the human race. And the human race is filled with passion. Medicine, law, business, engineering, these are noble pursuits and necessary to sustain life. But poetry, beauty, romance, love, these are what we stay alive for." — N.H. Kleinbaum, *Dead Poets' Society*

passion for poetry. Many leave their poetry unit until the month of June, turn to a reproducible poetry unit on Pinterest, and call it a day.

But why? Why is it that so many teachers don't enjoy teaching poetry? Lack of interest? Lack of confidence? Lack of understanding? My belief is that it is not due to a lack of interest or desire on the teacher's part, but more to do with the lack of knowing how. Whatever the reason, I'm hoping that this book brings a little inspiration, and that maybe you, too, will experience a passion for poetry, along with the many benefits it brings to your language instruction. It is my hope that, in reading it, some of that passion will begin to spill over into your classroom and that you, too, will come to understand that poetry needs a space and a place in all of our classrooms, not as a unit we teach but as a language we speak. Poetry lives in each of us. We just might need a little help finding it.

This book is intended to help your students experience the joy of hearing, reading, writing, and reciting poetry. It is divided into four "big idea" chapters: Discovering Poetry, Experiencing Poetry, Learning Poetry, and Creating Poetry. First, I present the big picture of poetry and outline ways to help your students discover just what poetry is. I delve into the sight, sound, feelings, and thoughts associated with poetry, emphasizing the fact that poetry is not simply another kind of writing, but that poems can change the way we look at things.

After introducing students to the big picture of poetry, I explore the experience of poetry. I outline practical ways that your students can experience the joy and playfulness of poetry in your classroom through a variety of poetry rituals. These rituals include listening to, reading, reciting, and responding to poetry. Other rituals include a Poem of the Week, a Poet-Tree corner, and Poetry Jams and Slams.

Before students can really begin creating their own poems, there are some specific lessons in poetic structure and devices that should be introduced. In the Learning Poetry section, I provide detailed lessons on seven poetic devices (simile, metaphor, personification, rhyming patterns, repetition, alliteration, and onomatopoeia) followed by a series of lessons introducing nine basic poetic structures (haiku, cinquain, list, acrostic, diamante, concrete, limerick, found poetry, and free verse). It is not my intention that you teach all of these lessons sequentially, but that you select ones that you feel best connect to your grade and the ability level of your students. As you will learn throughout this book, poetry is much more than structures and devices.

In the final section of this book, Creating Poetry, you will find lessons to help your students begin writing their own poems. Using the structure of Brain Pockets (Memory, Fact, and Imagination), I outline poetry lessons that can easily be integrated into your year plan and connect to topics you are already teaching. From writing metaphor poems about families, to an Animal Acrostic, to a Imaginary Creature poem, your students will begin to understand that poetry can be about anything, and that their memories, background knowledge, and imagination are their best resources. Each lesson clearly outlines the topic, target, structure, and anchor poems, and includes detailed instructions, teacher models, and student samples. The book ends with an outline for assessing poetry and my final thoughts.

My hope is that this book leaves you feeling more inspired and confident in your ability to sprinkle poetry joy into your classroom and help your students discover and experience the poems that are living inside each one of them.

"If you want to write poetry, you must have poems that deeply move you. Poems you can't live without. I think of a poem as the blood in a blood transfusion, given from the heart of the poet to the heart of the reader. Seek after poems that live inside you, poems that move through your veins." — Ralph Fletcher

Why *Not* Poetry?

"There is one kind of knowledge… infinitely precious,
time-resistant more than monuments, here to be
passed between the generations in any way it may be…
and that is poetry." — Mariel Rukeyser (1996, p. 13)

Many books I have read on teaching poetry begin with a chapter that tries to convince us that poetry has merit and value, and that it should be a part of every language arts program. Rather than trying to defend its value by asking, "Why poetry?" I tend to view the question as "Why NOT poetry?" Why would you not want your students to celebrate the rhythm, rhyme, and wordplay of a poem? Why would you not want to share the joy of poetry with your students and allow them to experience the sounds, sights, feelings, and thoughts connected to a poem? Why would you not want your students to be moved by a poem? Why would you not read poetry aloud to your students every day and allow them to listen to the way words can play and dance across a page? Why would you not teach poetic devices like metaphor or personification through poetry? Why would you not allow a poem to invite students' connections, questions, visual images, and inferences? Why would you not introduce your students to amazing poets and their poetry collections? (I love Shel Silverstein, too, but there are dozens of other great poets children need to know about!) Why not embed poetry in your students' day-to-day experiences?

Poetry is everywhere. It lives inside us but sometimes we don't recognize it because it doesn't rhyme or have a 5-7-5 syllable count. Not many teachers I speak to love teaching poetry. Feedback varies from "I don't have time" to "I don't know how." For those who do venture into doing a poetry unit, it often consists of a series of lessons on different poetic structures, such as acrostic, haiku, or cinquain. Students learn the structure, write a few poems, put their poems into a folder entitled My Poetry Anthology and hand it in for a mark. It is true that these teachers are "doing poetry," but they are not helping their students truly discover poetry in all its disguises and unlikely places.

Robert Pinsky says, "No instruction manual can teach as much as careful attention to the sounds in even one great poem" (1998, p. 7). No truer words have been spoken. If for no other reason than poems are short! It doesn't take much time to read a poem aloud and talk about it, to clap to the rhythm, to find the rhyming words, to notice a poetic device. But the benefits of those few moments spent with a poem go far beyond the few actual minutes you spend with it. Students who listen to poetry regularly become acquainted with poems, befriend them, find pleasure in them. They learn to find meaning in poetry, to make connections, draw inferences. And most importantly, students who listen to poetry regularly begin to recognize it in themselves. And once you have poetry inside you, there is no better way to get it out than to write it down.

Why poetry? Why NOT poetry? In summary, here are just a few reasons why poetry should live in every classroom.

"Poems, being short, are not demanding or frustrating to these readers. They can start them, finish them, and gain from them, without experiencing any discomfort whatsoever." — Lee Bennett Hopkins (1987, p.6)

Poetry...

- builds reading, writing, and speaking skills
- supports phonemic awareness; e.g., rhyming, syllables, etc.
- explores and celebrates words and language
- is visual, auditory, emotional, and cognitive
- inspires writing
- supports comprehension, meaning-making, connecting, visualizing, and inferring (Reading Power strategies)
- nurtures creativity, imagination, and feelings
- invites us to look at the world in a new way
- is FUN!

1 Discovering Poetry

"A great poem provides many simultaneous pleasures, which are also demands—that we hear, that we think, that we imagine, that we connect." — Lawrence Raab

What Is Poetry?

Before students start clapping syllables for their first haiku poem, we need to help them discover the true essence of poetry. Let's start by asking ourselves this question: What is poetry? What is the difference between a poem and a story? In simple terms, we could say a poem looks and sounds different from a story or prose. What makes it look different is the way it is formatted on the page, with shorter lines and more white space; what makes it sound different is that it includes at least one of three poetic elements (rhyme, repetition, and rhythm). Poems are often built from a specific structure (e.g., haiku, cinquain, acrostic) and include specific poetic devices (e.g., alliteration, personification, simile).

But ultimately, a poem is greater than the sum of its parts. A good poem isn't just words, white spaces, structure, and devices; it is a gift that the poet leaves behind for us—a feeling, a wonder, an image, a connection. A good poem doesn't end when we read the last line; a good poem lingers in our hearts and in our heads. Poetry is not simply another type of writing. A poem taps into all our senses and provides an experience that is both visual and auditory, emotional and cognitive. Poems look, sound, feel, and make us think differently than any other form of writing. This is what we want our students to discover about poetry, and leading them to this discovery is the first step in weaving poetry into your practice. Remember, poetry is not simply something we teach in isolation at the end of the year. We want poetry to live alongside our students and our literacy lessons all year.

The four lessons outlined here can be taught separately or combined into one.

Before launching into lessons about poetry structure or devices, I like to spend time discovering and exploring the big picture of poetry with my students. While students have heard the word *poetry* before, many are not able to articulate exactly what a poem is and how it differs from a story.

Lesson: What Does Poetry Look Like?

- Write the word *poetry* on the board. Ask students what the word means. Ask them to explain the difference between a poem and a story.
- Explain that you will be spending the next few minutes discussing what poetry is and how it's different from a story.

- Tell students that, first, you would like to focus on what poetry looks like. Hold up any open page of a novel. Ask students to describe what the page of a story looks like. (*lots of words going across the page; paragraphs; possibly dialogue*)

TEXT FORMS SAMPLE

Flying Popcorn

A piece of popcorn
escaped from the pan
and flew across the kitchen
like Superman.

It ping-ponged back and forth
between the oven and the freezer.
Then it shot up to the ceiling
like a daredevil trapeezer.

I tried and tried to catch it,
but it never missed a trick.
So finally I gave up
and ate a licorice stick.

- Hold up a page with a single poem written on it or project a poem onto a screen. Try to choose a poem that has specific stanzas and white spaces. Ask students to describe what they notice about the way a poem looks. (*has a title; shorter lines; fewer words; more white space;, sections, called stanzas*)
- Create a 4-square anchor chart called Discovering Poetry (see template on page 16). Add ideas into the first box, *What does poetry look like?* As you teach the other three lessons, you can add ideas into the remaining boxes.

SAMPLE DISCOVERING POETRY CHART

What does poetry look like?	What does poetry sound like?
Has a title *Shorter lines* *Fewer words* *More white spaces* *Stanzas*	
What does poetry feel like?	**What does poetry make us think about?**

Lesson: What Does Poetry Sound Like?

For this lesson, you will need a poem that includes many features of poetry, including a title, at least two stanzas, rhyming, repetition, and rhythm. While there are many to choose from, I like to use "Things" by Eloise Greenfield, a poem about a poem that includes all the poetic features I want to highlight.

Over time, the term "the 3 R's of Poetry" will become more and more familiar and provide a language with which to talk about any poem.

- Copy your chosen poem onto chart paper or have it ready to project onto a shared screen.
- Remind students that you are helping them discover a little more about what poetry is. You have already spent some time talking about what poetry looks like and how it is different from text you would find in a novel. (You might choose to introduce the term "prose" here.)
- Show or project the poem "Things" by Eloise Greenfield, or the poem you have chosen for the lesson. Review the features that make it "look" like a poem: title, stanzas, shorter lines, white spaces.
- Explain that you would like to focus on what a poem *sounds* like.
- Read the poem out loud and invite students to listen to the sound of the poem. Ask students what they noticed and discuss. *(some words rhyme; some words repeat; it has a beat; sounds like a song but with no music)*
- Write *The 3 R's* on the board. Explain that the term describes what a poem sounds like: Rhyme (when words in the poem sound the same), Repetition (when a word or phrase is written more than once), and Rhythm (when a poem has a beat).

    Not all poems have all three R's, but in order for something to be a called a poem, it needs to have at least one of the three R's.

- Read the poem again and invite students to pay attention to the three R's. Invite students to clap, snap, or tap if they notice a rhythm. Afterward, ask students to identify any rhyming words and repeating words or phrases.
- Add The 3 R's in the chart in the *What does poetry sound like?* box of the Discovering Poetry chart.
- Tell students that sometimes when you hear a poem, it almost sounds like a song but without the music. Add those ideas to the box on the chart.

Lesson: What Does Poetry Feel Like?

For this lesson, I use the same poem as I used in the preceding lesson: "Things" by Eloise Greenfield.

- Remind students that you are helping them discover poetry. Explain that you have been talking about what poetry looks like and sounds like. Tell students that we can see poetry and hear poetry, but we can also feel poetry.

    Poems often leave us with a feeling. A poem might make us laugh, or cry, or feel lonely, or get excited. Poems are magical in a way because, after the poem is finished, the feeling often stays with us. I like to say that sometimes "poetry lingers" in our hearts and in our heads after we finish reading it.

- Ask students what feeling they get when they read the poem "Things" by Elois Greenfield. *(happy, relaxed, hopeful, excited to write my own poem)*
- Add feeling words to the Discovering Poetry chart (see page 16).
- Read a few other poetry selections and invite students to think about how the poem makes them feel.

Lesson: What Does Poetry Make Us Think About?

- Remind students that poems are visual (we can see them), auditory (we can hear them), and emotional (we can feel them).
- Tell students that poems can sometimes make us think about things in new ways. Poems have meaning that we can think about.
- Refer back to the poem "Things" by Eloise Greenfield. Reread it and ask students what they think the poem means. Discuss (*sandcastles and candy don't last but a poem that you write does… so maybe we should all write poems!*).
- Explain that the poet wanted us to think about how poems last but she didn't actually write those words. She said something in a new way so we could think about it.
- Write the following poem on the whiteboard or on a shared screen:

  My Dog

  My dog is cute.
  My dog is fun.
  I love my dog.

- Read the poem aloud. Ask students: Does this look like a poem? (*yes—title, white space*) Does it have the 3 R's? (*yes—repetition*) Does it give you a feeling? (*poet says they love their dog*) Does it say something old in a new way? (*NO!*)
- Write the following poem on the white board or on a shared screen:

  My Dog

  My dog Poppy,
  Best dog Poppy,
  His tail tickles my legs
  His feet smell like wood chips.
  Best friend, Poppy.

- Read aloud and ask students similar questions. Discuss the fact that both poems are about dogs, but the second poem gives the reader more than just words and facts about a dog. There is a feeling, smell, a voice, and a lingering feeling that happens when we read it.

  Both poems are about a person who loves their dog, but each poet found a different way to say that. In the first poem, the poet actually writes those words and tells the reader directly that they love their dog. When a reader tells us something directly, we don't really need to think about it. In the second poem, the poet lets us know they love their dog without using those words. They say, "I love my dog" in a new way so it makes me think, "This person really loves their dog."

- Discuss what things poems might make us think about (*nature, family, friends, ourselves*). Complete the last box of the Discovering Poetry chart.

What does poetry look like?	What does poetry sound like?
Has a title	*Rhyme*
Shorter lines	*Repetition*
Fewer words	*Rhythm*
More white spaces	*Like a song without music*
Stanzas	
What does poetry feel like?	**What does poetry make us think about?**
Sad	*Nature*
Happy	*Things*
Lonely	*Ourselves*
Quiet	*Others*
Peaceful	*The world*
Excited	*Poems often say something old in a new way and can change the way we look at things.*
Poems linger—they give us many different feelings that stay behind.	

Below are more detailed explanations you may wish to use when explaining some of the descriptors in the Discovering Poetry chart.

- Poems have titles

    Yes, it's true! Just like stories, all poems have titles. When you write a poem, you must always include a title.

- Poems are written by poets

    Stories are written by authors; poems are written by poets. Poets always include their name on their poem, either at the bottom or under the title.

- Poems have short lines and white spaces

    Poems look different from stories. They have shorter lines that don't go across the full page and there is more white space on the page.

- Poems have sections called stanzas

    Writing is divided into sections called paragraphs; songs are divided into sections called verses; poems are divided into sections called stanzas. Like a paragraph or a verse, a stanza includes one main idea.

- Poems are like songs without music

    Sometimes when I read a poem, it reminds me of a song. Songs have verses, sometimes rhyme, often repeat words or phrases; give us feelings, just like poetry does. The only real difference between a poem and a song is the music!

- Poems include the 3 R's

  In order for a poem to be called a poem, it requires at least one of the following: rhyme, repetition, rhythm.

"The meaning of a poem is to stop time." — Ralph Fletcher

- Poems have meaning

  Poems have a lot of white spaces because the poet leaves room for our thinking! All poems mean something, but sometimes the meaning isn't written directly, only implied. For example, the poem "Things" is about how most "things" (that is, sandcastles and candy) don't last, but a poem is forever.

- Poems make pictures in our heads

  Many poems don't come with pictures or illustrations. Poetry is often filled with visually descriptive language and sensory details, so readers don't need a picture on the page because they can make pictures in their heads.

- Poems can be about anything

  You can write a poem about literally anything—from your baby brother, to polar bears, to unicorns! Poems are everywhere!

- Poems can sometimes tell a story

  Even though they have fewer words than a story, some poems tell stories.

- Poems give us feelings

  Poems can be funny or serious, soft or loud. Poems give us different feelings when we read them—happy, sad, scared, calm, free, excited, hopeful, grateful.

- Poems linger

  Poems can leave us with feelings and, sometimes, those feelings stay with us. That's what poetry can do—leave behind a feeling for us.

Anchor Books about Poetry

After introducing the concept of poetry to students, I like to follow up the lesson with a story or two featuring a character who discovers the joy of poetry living all around us. The following anchor books include some delightful poetry-loving characters:

Micha Archer, *Daniel Finds a Poem*
Sharon Creech, *Love That Dog*
Charles Ghigna, *A Poem is a Firefly*

Vern Kousky, *Otto the Owl Who Loved Poetry*
Randall Jarrell, *The Bat-Poet*
Margaret McNamara, *A Poem in Your Pocket*

Lesson: Finding Poems Where They Hide

For this lesson, you will need to bring in an object from nature that you discovered outside such as a leaf, a rock, or a twig. I spend a lot of time in the forest and in the trails. I use a pinecone for this lesson.

Poetry is not only a way of writing, but also a way of seeing. In addition to helping your students discover what a poem looks like, sounds like, and feels like, it's also important that you lead them to discover that poems are everywhere—we just have to use our "poet's eyes" to find them.

- Begin the lesson:

  Poets, we have been talking about the sights, sounds, feelings, and thoughts of poetry. Today, I want to talk about where we find poetry. Now, I know we could say that we find poetry in poetry books. But I mean, where do poets find poems? Take a moment and talk to your partner about where you think poems live.

- Students might not understand the question and could still answer "in a book." Some might say, "in nature"; others might say, "Poems are everywhere!" (Give that child a fist bump!) Continue to nudge them by asking: *Where do poets discover their poems?*
- Tell students that poems live everywhere!

  Poems are hiding everywhere! If you haven't discovered poetry yet, you won't know to look. But if you are a poet, you know that poems are everywhere; you just have to use your "poet's eyes" to look at the world. Poets are sometimes very still. Poets pay attention. They notice things. Poets see things that we see, but look at them in a different way. They use their poet's eyes to look at things. They might look at a pencil and discover a pencil poem living inside it; they might look at a cloud and see a poem floating across the sky.

- Tell students that you were walking in the forest and you noticed a pinecone on the trail. Explain that you have seen hundreds of pinecones before, but this time you decided to try to look at it with your poet's eyes. Tell them you picked up the pinecone and looked at it carefully. You were still. You paid attention. You noticed. All of a sudden, you discovered a pinecone poem—right there in the forest! Explain that because you knew what a poem looks like and sounds like, it was easier to find it.

I wrote this poem, but feel free to use it as your own.

- Read the poem aloud.

  Pinecone Poem by A. Gear

  Pinecone, pinecone
  On the forest floor
  Pinecone, pinecone
  Can't buy you in a store.

  Pinecone, pinecone
  Spikey brown scales
  Pinecone, pinecone,
  Marking up the trails.

  Pinecone, pinecone
  Not a cone to eat
  Pinecone, pinecone
  But such a forest treat.

You might have noticed that my poem sounds similar to "Things" by Eloise Greenfield, with a similar stanza count, rhythm, and rhyming pattern. If any student notices this, explain that reading poetry can help us when we write poetry. We can learn a lot from other poets.

- Discuss how this poem looks like a poem (three stanzas, shorter lines) and sounds like a poem (rhyme, repetition, rhythm).
- Explain to students that now that they have discovered what poetry looks like, sounds like, and feels like, they can start using their poet's eyes to see things a little differently. Encourage them to be still, pay attention, and look for poems everywhere.
- If possible, take students on a short walk to discover poems. Give them a clipboard and encourage them to be still, pay attention, and use their poet's eyes to discover poems everywhere!

The poem below was written completely independently by a student after this lesson. She told me she "used her poet's eyes" when she was looking at the grass in the park. I had not even taught the class personification yet, but there she is, talking to the grass in her poem! A wonderful example of discovering poetry. Feel free to share it with your students. (It's a lot better than my pinecone poem!)

STUDENT SAMPLE POEM

Grade 1

grass

grass oH grass
In sprintim
you tikl my toes.

grass ott grass
In summr
you scrach my legs.

grass ott grass
I like tikles BeTTr.

By Lily

2 Experiencing Poetry

"Every writer of poetry is first a reader of poetry."
— Georgia Heard (1999, p. 1)

After introducing the sights, sounds, feelings, and thoughts of poetry, it's time to bring on the poetry joy! While often our goal is to have our students write their own poetry, and while most students can follow a 5-7-5 syllable count and say they have written a haiku, in order for students to write poetry with any semblance of feeling or thought, they must experience it first. It's that simple. Pinterest poetry units, grounded in a variety of poetic structures for your students to follow—one haiku, two cinquain, three acrostic, done—rarely mention the poetry experience. So, before you start teaching metaphors or diamantes, let poetry fill your classroom! Let your students hear it, feel it, snap to it, clap to it, breathe it in, let it linger. Passion breeds passion, so get excited about poetry! Be the teacher your students will always remember as being the one who brought poetry to life for them. Read it, recite it, rejoice in it, be moved by it. It won't take long before your students are doing the same.

Establishing Poetry Rituals

Once we make the shift in our thinking that poetry isn't just something we *fit in* but something we *live in*, poetry becomes a natural addition to our day-to-day practice. When we make poetry visible in our classrooms and establish regular poetry routines and rituals, we can help students develop a lasting friendship with it. Here are some suggestions of bringing the poetry experience to life in your classroom.

Poetry Every Day in Every Way!

- Read! Read! Read! lots of poems every day
- Poetry Books: fill your classroom with poetry books, anthologies, etc.
- Make Poetry Fun through Poetry Jams and Slams!
- Read Stories featuring poetry-loving characters
- Make a Poet-Tree: create a poetry corner in your class, complete with a Poet-Tree
- Poetry Mentors: introduce students to many different children's poets; feature a new one each month
- Link Poetry to Content Areas: science, social studies, art, math, music

---

Read! Read! Read!

"It's what you hear that makes your heart thump or makes you feel a little giddy and out of breath." — Scott Elledge (1990, xviii)

Many poems move, sing, and sway, but the rhythm and cadence come alive only when a poem is read aloud. Sharing poems with your students on a regular basis will help them become acquainted with the movement and playfulness found in poems. We all know that passion is contagious. Showing and sharing excitement and enthusiasm for poetry will inspire your students, and soon the whole class will be swaying, snapping, and clapping in time to the rhythm. Besides being a one-stop literacy lesson, many children's poems are chock-a-block full of giggle-launching silliness! Providing time and space in your class for poems to live, be celebrated, and enjoyed will create a joyful noise in your classroom. Make poetry fun! Read different kinds of poems at different times of the day and for different reasons. Read funny poems, quiet poems, sad poems, memory-pocket poems, fact-pocket poems, and imagination-pocket poems. Immerse your students in the joyful sound of poetry every day.

See Chapter 4 for more on Brain Pocket poetry.

Fill Your Classroom with Poetry

Poetry Partners is a fun way to encourage students to read poems to each other once a week. Poetry Partners can be easily integrated into The Daily 5 ("Read to Someone") or Buddy Reading.

Do a quick survey of your classroom library—how many poetry books do you have? If the answer is "none," "a few," or "I don't know," it's time to get some! There are hundreds of outstanding poetry books for children (besides *Where the Sidewalk Ends*!). I recommend setting up a Poetry Corner consisting of a "table with a label" (I love rhymes!) and fill it with poetry collections and anthologies. Rotate the books, bringing in different collections connected to seasons, celebrations, and topics connected to your content areas. Poetry anthologies are great for this table because each includes a variety of structures, topics, and poets. Encourage students to choose a poetry book for independent reading or shared reading time.

Favorite Poetry Anthologies

Booth, David, ed. *'Til All the Stars Have Fallen: Canadian Poems for Children*

Prelutsky, Jack, ed. *The 20th Century Children's Poetry Treasury*

Prelutsky, Jack, ed. *The Random House Book of Poetry for Children*

Prelutsky, Jack, ed. *Read-Aloud Rhymes for the Very Young*

Schenk de Regniers, Beatrice, ed. *Sing a Song of Popcorn: Every Child's Book of Poems*

Stevens, Roger, ed. *A Million Brilliant Poems: The Best Children's Poetry Today (Part One)*

Yolen, Jane, ed. *Here's a Little Poem: A Very First Book of Poetry*

Reciting Poetry

Memorizing poetry fills up students with patterns of language. When students start writing their own poems, these patterns will spill back out. Speaking the words of a poem is equally important to listening to them. Somehow, when we speak and repeat words of a poem, they stick. Many of us can rattle off any number of nursery rhymes by heart; I still remember the words to poems I memorized and recited in high school. There is something quite satisfying about reciting a poem now that I learned when I was 16. And while I don't ever want students to equate poetry with the stress of memorizing and reciting, I do believe giving students the opportunity to recite and perform poetry can be beneficial.

Experiencing the word play, rhythm, and repetition first-hand as it emerges from your own mouth has a more lasting impact than listening to someone else read. It's important to provide regular opportunities for your students to read, recite, and perform poems for the sheer joy of it, with no pressure of being "marked." Here are two ways to invite students to participate in reciting poetry.

Poetry Jam

A Poetry Jam is a fun way to play with a poem through repetitive class participation. Choose a simple, lively poem that has a lot of rhythm and repetition and two to four stanzas (see recommendations below). Poems specifically for two voices work really well for this activity.

- Copy the poem, using different colors for different stanzas or voices.
- Read the poem aloud to the class.
- Invite students to read it with you; repeat several times.
- Assign different stanzas to different individuals or small groups (I assign only to students who volunteer).
- Introduce creative ways to read aloud: whispering parts; dividing the class in smaller groups; standing when it's your turn to read; adding actions—be creative!
- By the time you are finished, most of your students will know the poem by heart, and some might wish to compete in a Poetry Slam!

Poetry Slam

Poetry Slams are poetry competitions in which poets read or recite original poems with great flair. A modified version of a slam can be an engaging way for individual students to perform a poem. Using the same poem that you used for the class Poetry Jam, students can participate in a lively Poetry Slam!

- Choose two or three students who volunteer to participate.
- Using the poem learned during the Poetry Jam, students stand and "perform" the poem. Encourage creativity, movement, gestures, expression, flair, vigor, and a little swag!
- Poetry Slam presentations can be performed throughout the week.

Often, I allow a few minutes for students to practice their performance in the hallway or coat room before they perform.

Poetry Collections Recommended for Poetry Jams and Poetry Slams

Donaldson, Julia. *Poems to Perform*
Fleischman, Paul. *Joyful Noise: Poems for Two Voices*
Hale, Glorya. *Read-Aloud Poems: 50 of the World's Best-Loved Poems for Parent and Child to Share*
Heard, Georgia. *Boom! Bellow! Bleat! Animal Poems for Two or More Voices*
Heidbreder, Robert. *Don't Eat Spiders*

Hoberman, Mary Ann. *Forget-Me-Nots: Poems to Learn by Heart*
Hoberman, Mary Ann. *You Read to Me, I'll Read to You: Very Short Stories to Read Together*
Kennedy, Caroline. *Poems to Learn by Heart*
Stevens, Roger. *Off by Heart: Poems for Children to Learn and YOU to Remember*

Poetry as a Presence in Your Classroom

Poet-Tree

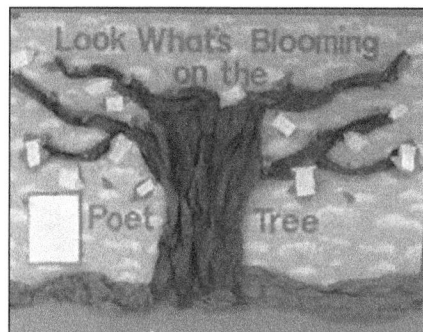

Giving poetry a permanent home in your classroom helps to reinforce its value. One idea I have used is creating a poetry corner that includes a Poet-Tree display on one of the walls (see photos above). On the paper cut-out tree, you can hang copies of different poems for students to "pick," students' poetry, or poetry by a featured Poet of the Week. Adding floor cushions can create a inviting place for students to come to read or share poetry.

Poem in Your Pocket

"A Poem in Your Pocket" by Margaret McNamara and the new book *Poem in My Pocket* by Chris Tougas would make excellent anchor books to launch Poem in Your Pocket Day!

Believe it or not, there is actually a national Poem in Your Pocket Day! It falls during National Poetry Month in April, prompted by an international movement that encourages you to select a favorite poem and carry it with you, sharing it at school, at home, at the park, in the coffee shop—basically everywhere you go! What fun to do this with your class! On PIYP Day, invite every student to choose a poem, copy it, and keep it in their pocket for the day. They can share it with their classmates, with other teachers, with their buddies, on the playground, with their family, etc. The movement even has its own hashtag: #PocketPoem

Request-a-Poem Jar

Encourage students to request poems they would like to you to read. Set up a Poetry Request Jar on your desk or on the poetry table. Students can request a specific poem, poet, or topic by writing it on a slip of paper and adding it to the jar.

Including names on their requests is optional, but if a name is included, I like to start my poetry sharing with, "Today's poem is a request from_____." This helps grow a feeling of poetry pride, as students' requests are shared with everyone. Often students request poems we have already read or discussed as a class, reminding us that it doesn't take long for students to start developing a preference for favorite poems and poets.

Poets Corner

When asked, "Who is your favorite's children's poet?" most teachers will respond, "Shel Silverstein." And while there is no doubt that Mr. Silverstein has brought poetry delight to thousands of children and adults, and earned his place as one of the most beloved children's poets of all time, he is but one of many poets we should be sharing and celebrating with our students. Students' experience of poetry can include being introduced to the diversity and voices of extraordinary children's poets. Putting a face to a name can help make the poems we share come alive. I love it when a student makes a connection to a poet they know or comes up to me and says, "Look, Ms. Gear! I found a poem by…" It can be as simple as setting up a Poets Corner in your classroom and featuring different poets throughout the year.

- Choose a featured poet (see list below).
- Print off the poet's photograph (many are available on the Internet) and post it on a wall or bulletin board.
- Identify them by their full name.
- Include a short bio: date and place of birth, etc.
- Print and post poems by the featured poet for students to read.
- Hang copies of the poet's poems on your Poet-Tree.
- Set up a table to display some of the featured poet's poetry books.
- Read aloud some of the featured poet's poems

KNOW IT — THE POET!

This list of recommended children's poets and their featured poetry books is not comprehensive, but it should give you a good start.

Douglas Florian
Best known for clever poems about science, nature, and seasons:

In the Swim
Insectlopedia
Autumnblings
Comets, Stars, the Moon, and Mars
Beast Feast

Eloise Greenfield
Best known for depiction of African American experience, particularly family life:

Honey, I Love
In the Land of Words
Under the Sunday Tree

Nikki Grimes
Best known for storytelling poems for older students, tough topics, lyrical phrasing, poetic devices:

Poems in the Attic
One Last Word
A Pocketful of Poems
Words with Wings

Robert Heidbreder
Canadian; retired Kindergarten teacher; known for his rhythmic, rhyming poems about family, community, and country:

Don't Eat Spiders
Eenie Meenie Manitoba
See Saw Saskatchewan
Noisy Poems for a Busy Day

Langston Hughes
Known for jazz rhythm, the Black experience, social justice issues:

The Sweet and Sour Animal Book
My People
Poetry for Young People

Dennis Lee
Canadian; known for humor, strong rhythms, musical sounds, repetition, easy-to-remember poems:

Alligator Pie
Garbage Delight
The Ice Cream Store

Kenn Nesbitt
Best known for his silly (bathroom) humor and relatable subjects:

My Cat Knows Karate: Funny Poems for Kids
The Biggest Burp Ever: Funny Poems for Kids
The Tighty Whitey Spider and More Wacky Animal Poems I Totally Made Up
When the Teacher Isn't Looking and Other Funny School Poems

Naomi Shihabe Nye
Best known for poetry for upper and middle grades, thought-provoking, fresh look at ordinary events:

Honeybee
Voices in the Air
Everything Comes Next

Jack Prelutsky
Known for imagination, humor, celebrations:

Be Glad Your Nose Is on Your Face And Other Poems
It's Raining Pigs and Noodles
Something Big Has Been Here
Scranimals

Joyce Sidman
Best known for poems of science, nature, and animals, and use of poetic devices, such as personification and similes:

Red Sings from Treetops
Winter Bees
Swirl By Swirl

Song of the Water Boatman
This is Just to Say: Poems of Apology and Forgiveness

Shel Silverstein
Known for his quirky humor, wit, cartoons, and relatable subjects:

Where the Sidewalk Ends
A Light in the Attic

Marilyn Singer
Best known for nonfiction poetry, poems connected to science and nature, beautiful word choice:

Turtle in July
A Strange Place to Call Home
A Stick is an Excellent Thing
The Company of Crows

Amy Ludwig VanDerwater
Known for her joy in words and for finding poems in simple, everyday events and objects:

Write! Write! Write!
Read! Read! Read!
With My Hands: Poems About Making Things

Valerie Worth
Best known for simple free verse, poems about and personifying small objects:

All the Small Poems and Fourteen More
Animal Poems
Pug and Other Animal Poems

DON'T FORGET THE CLASSICS!

Poetry for Young People: Maya Angelou
Poetry for Young People: Lewis Carroll
Poetry for Young People: Emily Dickinson
Poetry for Young People: Robert Frost
Poetry for Young People: Langston Hughes
Poetry for Young People: Rudyard Kipling
Poetry for Young People: Edgar Allen Poe
Poetry for Young People: William Shakespeare
A Child's Garden of Verses: Robert Louis Stevenson
Poetry for Young People: Walt Whitman

Poem of the Week

If weekly feels like too much for you, every second week or once a month works just as well!

Poems are short, but oh, so rich with teachable features! Chart paper or a screen bearing a carefully selected poem can provide you with enough fluency, comprehension, and writing lessons to last a week! From rhyming to rhythm, from making connections to inferring, from simile to metaphor, from haiku to onomatopoeia, you can find everything you need for your literacy lesson at your fingertips within a few lines or stanzas of a good poem.

One of the easiest ways for your students to experience poetry is by establishing a Poem of the Week ritual. Besides the sheer pleasure of sharing great poems with students, a poem of the week also provides

- a link between reading and writing
- an introduction to different poetic devices and structures within the context of a real poem
- a short text for practicing Reading Power strategies (connecting, questioning, visualizing, inferring, transforming)
- an opportunity for students to read, write, recite, and perform poetry.
- an opportunity for students to respond to poetry both orally and in writing

When choosing my weekly poem, I often work backwards from the specific structure, poetic feature, or poetic device I am planning to teach later that week. For example, if I'm going to be introducing metaphors, I might choose *December Leaves* by Kaye Starbird for the poem of the week because it is rich with metaphors. If I'm introducing onomatopoeia, I will share *Weather Is Full of the Nicest Sounds* by Aileen Fisher because of the extensive list of sound words. But other times (when I may not be so organized!), I simply choose a poem because it's fun!

The chart below includes some of my favorite choices for Poem of the Week and teachable features—poetic devices and structures—featured in each.

If you aren't able to find these poems in books, many of these are available on the internet and YouTube.

RECOMMENDED POEM-OF-THE-WEEK POEMS

Poem	Teachable Features
"A Book" by Myra Cohn Livingston	Personification Infer meaning: books are friends
"April Rain Song" by Langston Hughes	Repetition Personification Feelings: calm, peaceful, grateful
"Autumn Leaves" by Aileen Fisher	Rhyme Visualizing Senses
"Drinking Fountain" by Marchette Chute	Rhyme Rhythm Humor Visualizing
"Fog" by Carl Sandburg	Metaphor Personification
"I Loved My Friend" by Langston Hughes	Feelings: sad, lonely Free verse
"I Wandered, Lonely as a Cloud" by William Wordsworth	Simile Rhyming pattern Visual images

"March" by Enola Chamberlin	Rhyme pattern Personification
"Mine" by Lillian Moore	Rhyme Rhythm Repetition Personification
"Recess" by Avis Harley	Onomatopoeia
"Spring Splashdown" by Joyce Sidman	Repetition Alliteration
"Stopping by the Woods on a Snowy Evening" by Robert Frost	Visualizing Repetition Feelings: peaceful, tranquil, calm
"Things" by Eloise Greenfeld	Repetition Rhyme Rhythm Infer meaning: poems last forever
"This Tooth" by Lee Bennett Hopkins	Alliteration Repetition Rhyme Stanzas Connecting
"Weather is full of the Nicest Sounds" by Aileen Fisher	Onomatopoeia Surprise ending
"When Skies are Low" by N.M. Bodecker	Rhyme Simile Word choice Visual images
"White Sheep, White Sheep" by Christina Rossetti	Metaphor Repetition Rhyme
"Whispers" by Myra Cohn Livingston	Repetition Rhyme Rhythm Personification Feelings: calm, quiet

My "go to" site for examples of literary devices in well-known poems is https://literarydevices.net/

Once you have selected a poem, copy it onto chart paper or project it on a shared screen. Always try to have a copy of the poem visible for students, either on a chart stand or on a shared photocopy. It's important for students to be able to see a poem as well as hear it, so they can see the formatting and identify features such as rhyme, repeating words and phrases, and poetic devices.

Poem of the Week Routine

- Introduce the poem:

  Our Poem of the Week is called _____, and it's by the poet_____.

- Invite students to listen for the 3 R's while you read. Read the poem aloud once.
- Read the poem a second time, inviting students to join in if they wish to.
- Invite some students to help identify the rhyming words and repetitive phrases (if applicable); discuss if there is a beat.

See *Reading Power* (Gear, 2015) for more on Reading Power strategies.

- Apply any Reading Power strategies you might be focusing on: *What connections did you make? What visual images did this poem give you?*
- Discuss the meaning of the poem and invite students to share their thoughts and "maybes" (inferences).
- Discuss what feeling the poem gives readers.
- Ask students what their favorite word, part, or sound was.
- Notice aloud any poetry devices they may already know (similes, personification, etc.)
- If you are using the poem to teach a specific feature (e.g., metaphor, personification, etc.) introduce it and show how the poet uses it in the poem.
- End the lesson by reading the poem together with students one last time. Invite individual students to read aloud.

Responding to the Poem of the Week

There is no one right answer when it comes to poetry. Providing time for students to respond to poetry helps build comprehension and reinforce that poems have meaning. It also encourages them to share parts of poems they liked, words they noticed, and feelings they experienced when reading poetry. So much about a poem is what is *not* written that poems provide excellent resources for practicing such strategies as making connections, visualizing, and making inferences. Responses to the Poem of the Week can be written, oral, or a combination.

WRITTEN RESPONSES

How much time you spend on Poem of the Week is up to you, but I might introduce the poem of the week one day and then revisit the poem later in the week and have students work on a written response. Depending on what grade you teach, you might wish to use a structured template or a more open-ended prompt format; see examples that follow.

- Structured Response Template
A structured template for written responses to the Poem of the Week works for students who are just beginning to develop different ways of responding to a poem; see Poetry Response template on pages 34–35. The headings on the boxes can change, depending on what poetic features or comprehension strategies are being focused on; see samples on page 30.

Familiarizing Format

On one side of the response sheet, I provide space and lines for students to copy the poem (see page 34). Note that I do not promote students sitting quietly in their desks doing "printing practice" by copying line after line of perfect poetry. I look at this more as a practice for formatting. When students are beginning to write poetry but are not familiar with the shorter lines, often they continue writing to the end of the line and their poem ends up looking more like a story. In my experience, students need time to become familiar with the formatting, lines, and spaces of a poem. I invite them to choose their favorite stanza from the Poem of the Week to copy. I emphasize the title and poet's name, and encourage them to use the same formatting and spacing as the original. Once students become more familiar with the way a poem is written, the easier it is for them to format their own poems.

When introducing the response sheet, it is best to model your expectations for each of the four boxes. For students familiar with Reading Power strategies, making connections and visualizing will be something they can easily apply to poetry.

STUDENT SAMPLE: POETRY RESPONSE

Poetry Response

This poem reminds me of
Big puddles and I am stomping at it.

This is the picture I have in my mind when I read this poem:

Here are my favorite words from this poem:
gray
hours
showers
windy

Here are some feeling words I have when I read this poem:
happy
sad
Glad

March
By Enola Chamberlin

March is sometimes
wet with showers;
Bright sometimes
With sunny hours;
Sometimes windy,
Sometimes gray.
Yet I'm glad
she come my way.

• Open-Ended Prompts

For those who prefer a more open-ended response format, the chart below provides students with prompts for responding to the Poem of the Week. Students can select one or two prompts and use them to write about the Poem of the Week in a Poetry Response notebook. Again, teacher modeling is important to ensure your students know how to develop their ideas with details and examples. This chart could be posted in the classroom or students could glue it in their notebook.

When I read this poem

I notice…

It makes me think about…

It reminds me of…

I'm wondering…

I can really visualize…

I like the part ….

This part makes me feel…

I think the poet means…

I'm wondering if anyone else thought …

It reminds me of another poem…

This part makes me feel/think/wonder…

I like the sound of ….

I like the way the poet ….

ORAL RESPONSES

While written responses are important, written output is rarely a reflection of cognitive ability. Not all students can express their ideas or thoughts clearly when asked to write. As an alternative to a written response to the Poem of the Week, provide time for students to discuss the poem, either as a whole class or in partners, using the same prompts listed above. Remember to always model your own responses out loud, so students hear the language for responding to poems. After modeling, invite students to choose a prompt and use it to discuss the poem with a partner. Walk around the room, lean in and listen to the discussions. Provide tips and encouragement, and invite some students to share their thinking with the class.

Poetry and Reading Power

Because of the limited words and use of figurative language, poetry can often require deeper comprehension strategies. Those of you familiar with the comprehension strategies in my Reading Power books can see how well they can be applied to reading and responding to poetry. If you are teaching Making Connections, why not use a poem one day instead of a story? When teaching Inferring, a poem is a perfect source for noticing what the poet is implying. When teaching Visualizing, poetry is a perfect invitation to focus on sensory details that help paint a picture in the reader's mind. Here is a list of strategies and prompts that students can use when thinking through a poem.

Making Connections: "This part of the poem reminds me of…"

Visualizing: "When I read the part where _____, I could see _____ in my mind."

Questioning: "I'm wondering…"

Inferring: "Maybe when the poet says _____, they mean…"

Transforming: "This poem makes me think about _____ in a new way."

Retelling: "This poem is about…"

Connecting Poetry to Content

When students see poetry being integrated into content areas, their poetry experience expands. I love linking poetry to the content I am teaching and, from what I have discovered, there is a poem for just about everything! It's just a matter of finding it. Here are some suggestions for poetry books to link to your content areas:

Poems About School

Dakos, Kalli. *If You're Not Here, Please Raise Your Hand: Poems About School*

Salas, Laura Purdie. *Do Buses Eat Kids? Poems About School*

Shields, Carol Diggory. *After the Bell Rings: Poems About After-School Time*

Shields, Carol Diggory. *Lunch Money and Other Poems About School*

Winters, Kay. *Did You Hear What I Heard? Poems About School*

Poems About Math

Franco, Betsy. *Mathematickles!*

Franco, Betsy. *Math Poetry: Linking Language and Math in a Fresh Way*

Hopkins, Lee Bennett. *Marvelous Math: A Book of Poems*

Ziefert, Harriet. *Mother Goose Math*

Poems About Science

Scieszka, Jon, and Smith, Lane. *Science Verse*

Whitman, Walt. *When I Heard the Learn'd Astronomer*

Winters, Kari-Lynn. *Hungry for Science: Poems to Crunch On*

POEMS ABOUT ANIMALS

Brown, Skila. *Slickety Quick: Poems about Sharks*

Davies, Nicola. *Song of the Wild: A First Book of Animals*

Florian, Douglas. *Beast Feast*

Florian, Douglas. *Insectlopedia*

Florian, Douglas. *In the Swim*

Harrison, David L. *After Dark: Poems about Nocturnal Animals*

Singer, Marilyn. *The Company of Crows*

Singer, Marilyn. *A Strange Place to Call Home: The World's Most Dangerous Habitats and the Animals that Call them Home*

Singer, Marilyn. *Turtle in July*

Worth, Valerie. *Animal Poems*

POEMS ABOUT NATURE

Davies, Nicola. *A First Book of the Sea*

Davies. Nicola. *Outside Your Window: A First Book of Nature*

Elliott, David. *In the Past: From Trilobites to Dinosaurs to Mammoths in More Than 500 Million Years*

Harrison, David L. *The Dirt Book: Poems About Animals That Live Beneath Our Feet*

Holmer, Anders. *Rain*

Kapchinske, Pam. *Hey Diddle Diddle: A Food Chain Tale*

Lewis, J. Patrick, ed. *National Geographic Book of Nature Poetry*

Sidman, Joyce. *Butterfly Eyes and Other Secrets of the Meadow*

Sidman, Joyce. *Dark Emperor and Other Poems of the Night*

Sidman, Joyce. *Song of the Water Boatman and Other Pond Poems*

Sidman, Joyce. *Winter Bees and Other Poems of the Cold*

Singer, Marilyn. *A Stick Is an Excellent Thing: Poems Celebrating Outdoor Play*

Tuttle, Sarah Grace. *Hidden City: Poems of Urban Wildlife*

POEMS ABOUT SEASONAL CHANGES

Florian, Douglas. *Handsprings* (see also *Autumblings, Winter Eyes, Summersaults*)

Fogliano, Julie. *When Green Becomes Tomatoes: Poems for All Seasons*

Janeczko, Paul B. *Firefly July: A Year of Very Short Poems*

Prelutsky, Jack. *It's Snowing! It's Snowing! Winter Poems*

Sidman, Joyce. *Red Sings from Treetops: A Year in Colors*

Waters, Fiona, ed. *Sing a Song of Seasons: A Nature Poem for Each Day of the Year*

Zolotow, Charlotte. *Changes: A Child's First Poetry Collection*

POEMS ABOUT SPACE

Florian, Douglas. *Comets, Stars, the Moon, and Mars*

Sklansky, Amy B. *Out of This World: Poems and Facts About Space*

Whitman, Walt. *When I Heard the Learn'd Astronomer*

Poems About Social Studies

POEMS ABOUT CULTURE, CELEBRATIONS, AND FESTIVALS

Chatterjee, Debjani, and D'Arcy, Brian, eds. *Let's Celebrate: Festival Poems from Around the World*

Khan, Hena. *Golden Domes and Silver Lanterns: A Muslim Book of Colors*

Larios, Julie. *Delicious! Poems Celebrating Street Food Around the World*

Lewis, J. Patrick. *World Rat Day: Poems About Real Holidays You've Never Heard Of*

Livingston, Myra Cohn. *Birthday Poems*

Peters, Andrew Fusek. *The Chinese Dragon and Other Poems About Festivals*

Prelutsky, Jack. *It's Halloween* (see also *It's Thanksgiving, It's Valentine's Day, It's Christmas*)

Singer, Marilyn. *Every Month Is a New Year: Celebrations Around the World*

Singer, Marilyn. *Follow the Recipe: Poems about Imagination, Celebration, and Cake*

Wright, Danielle, ed. *My Village: Rhymes from Around the World*

POEMS ABOUT THE EARTH

Cooling, Wendy, ed. *All the Wild Wonders: Poems of Our Earth*

Glaser, Linda. *Our Big Home: An Earth Poem*

Nicholls, Judith. *The Barefoot Book of Earth Poems*

Sidman, Joyce. *Hello, Earth! Poems to Our Planet*

Walker, Sally M. *Earth Verse: Haiku From the Ground Up*

POEMS ABOUT FAMILY

Alarcón, Francisco. *Family Poems for Every Day of the Week*

Curry, Jennifer, ed. *Family Poems*

Greenfield, Eloise. *Brothers and Sisters: Family Poems*

Hoberman, Mary Ann. *Fathers, Mothers, Sisters, Brothers: A Collection of Family Poems*

Smith, Hope Anita. *My Daddy Rules the World: Poems About Dads*

POEMS ABOUT FRIENDS

Florian, Douglas. *Friends and Foes: Poems About Us All*

Latham, Irene, and Waters, Charles. *Can I Touch Your Hair? Poems of Race, Mistakes, and Friendship*

Livingston, Myra Cohn. *A Time to Talk: Poems of Friendship*

Lumb, Anna. *Cloud Making Friends: Children's Poetry Book about Friendship, Self Esteem & Self-Confidence*

Sidman, Joyce. *This Is Just to Say: Poems of Apology and Forgiveness*

POEMS ABOUT SPORTS AND PLAY

Florian, Douglas. *Play, Play, Play*

Florian, Douglas. *Poem Run: Baseball Poems and Paintings*

Heidbreder, Robert. *Crocodiles Play!*

Hopkins, Lee Bennett. *Sports! Sports! Sports! A Poetry Collection*

Steinglass, Elizabeth. *Soccerverse: Poems about Soccer*

van de Vendel, Edward. *I'll Root for You and Other Poems*

Poetry Response: Side 1

Name: _____

Title: _____

Poet: _____

_____

_____

_____

_____

_____

_____

_____

_____

_____

_____

_____

_____

_____

Poetry Response: Side 2

Poem: _____   Poet: _____

This poem is about…	This poem reminds me of…
_____	_____
_____	_____
_____	_____
_____	**This poem makes me think about…**
_____	_____
_____	_____

When I read this poem, I visualize:	The 3 R's
	Rhyming words?
	_____
	_____
	Repeating words?
	_____
	_____
	Rhythm? Yes/No
	My favorite word or phrase:
	_____
	_____

Pembroke Publishers © 2021 *Powerful Poetry* by Adrienne Gear ISBN 978-1-55138-352-1

3 Learning Poetry

"Poetry is ordinary language raised to the Nth power. Poetry is boned with ideas, nerved and blooded with emotions, all held together by the delicate, tough skin of words." — Paul Engle

If I show up at a hockey game with a stick and puck but have never held a stick, shot a puck, or learned the rules, I will likely not get much ice time. I may know how to skate, but in order to play hockey, I need to learn the skills and the rules of the game and I need to spend time practicing. Writing poetry is no different. If I show up ready to write a poem with my pencil in hand and my blank paper in front of me, I may know how to print, but without knowing the rules or the skills of poetry, I will not be successful.

There is no getting around the fact that teaching poetry requires some explicit instruction in both poetic structures and devices. Children will not get better at writing poems without learning the ways in which poetic structure and language are used to construct and enhance a poem. If you are familiar with any of my Writing Power books, you will know that my "secret sauce" for a successful writing program is explicit instruction, combined with lots of time for application. Students will need specific targeted instruction in poetic structure and language, along with time to apply and practice, in order to be successful poets.

When I teach poetry, I like to focus on a particular poetic structure (e.g., haiku, acrostic, list poem) then combine that with a specific target, or poetic device (e.g., alliteration, personification, metaphor) to be applied when students are working on their weekly practice poem. It is not my intention that you teach these poetic devices in isolation one after another, but rather that you teach one in the context of a poetic structure. For example, you could introduce students to the poetic device of alliteration. Later, they will apply alliteration when they are practicing writing Noisy Poems (see page 111). Once students know the poetic device, they can apply it to a wide range of poetic structures and topics.

In this book, I have provided mini lessons for seven poetic devices and eight poetic structures. Once students have some experience and understanding of the different poetic structures and techniques, they are better equipped to write their own poems, and the structures and devices can be mixed-and-matched in endless combinations.

I have found this website very helpful for teaching poetic devices. https://storytrail.com/poetry/poeticdevices_elementary.htm

Poetic Devices

"A figure of speech is not just an ornament that a poet attaches to a poem the way people put glass balls on Christmas trees." — Ted Kooser (2005, 125)

Poetic devices are essential tools a poet uses to create rhythm, enhance a poem's meaning, or intensify an image, mood, or feeling. To me, they give a poem personality. Teaching them is an important part of a poetry unit, but what's also important is to understand that once poetic devices are taught, students need to practice them in context by incorporating them into a poem. Writing isolated similes and displaying them on the bulletin board might be good practice, but might leave us questioning what they are for. Poetic devices alone do nothing. They need a home in a poem (now there's a great rhyme you can use!). We need to make it clear: poetic devices help make our poems better, so we need to include them when we write poetry!

While there are more than two dozen poetic devices to choose from, I am sharing the seven I find are featured most in children's poetry:

- **Simile**: comparing two things using a connecting word *like* or *as*
- **Metaphor**: comparing two things without using connecting words
- **Personification:** writing about an object as if it was a person
- **Repetition:** repeating words or phrases for effect
- **Rhyming Patterns**: the last word in the line rhymes with the last word of another line
- **Alliteration**: repeating the same sound; e.g., *Snakes slither silently.*
- **Onomatopoeia**: using words that make the sound of what they mean; e.g., *Pop! Beep! Swish!*

Simile

A simile is a literary device that directly compares two things using one of the connecting words *as* or *like*. Writers often use similes to make a description more vivid. I have found teaching students how to write similes transforms their writing more quickly and easily than any other technique. The trick is to ensure that the similes enhance the idea, not take away from it. A simile is a writing technique that can be used in narrative and story writing as well as poetry, so those who have used my Writing Power books will be familiar with this technique.

ANCHOR POEMS FOR TEACHING SIMILE

"When Skies are Low" by N.M. Bodecker
"My Dragon" by A. Gear (see lesson)
"Moon" by Nikki Grimes
"I Wandered, Lonely as a Cloud" by William Wordsworth

LESSON

- Begin the lesson:

  Poets, today, I'm going to show you a simple technique that poets often use to make their poems more interesting. Here is an example of a poet that used this technique in their poem.

The four poetic devices I find students can apply easily to their own poems are repetition, alliteration, personification, and simile. I use a lot of acronyms in my teaching, so RAPS is the acronym I use to remind students to add some poetic devices to their poem: "Make sure your poem *RAPS!*"

- Read the poem that includes similes:

My Dragon by A. Gear

My dragon's eyes are round like plates
Its teeth are sharp as knives,
Its open mouth like blackened caves
Its scales like large beehives.

Its mouth lets out a plume of smoke
It looks just like a chimney
Its body huge, like a giant whale
Its tail is long and skinny.

Its tongue flicks like an angry cat
Its claws a pointed needle
But dragon's sweet like candy floss
Not mean, or bad, or evil.

- Briefly discuss the 3 R's and discuss the three stanzas.
- Tell students that this poem is very descriptive and helps the reader visualize what the dragon looks like. Ask students if they noticed anything interesting that the poet was doing in their description.
- Write the word *simile* on the board. Explain:

    A simile is used when an author describes something by comparing it to something "similar," using the word like *or* as. *Similes help readers visualize. If I write, "His eyes are round," not too much happens in your brain. But if I write, "His eyes are round like plates," all of a sudden, you start to visualize eyes that are big and round like dinner plates.*

- Invite students to identify other similes in the dragon poem. Ask which one helped them "see a picture in their mind." Tell students that many poets use similes in their poems to help their reader to "see" the poem more clearly.
- Practice writing similes with the class by asking them to think of a time when they felt very hot; e.g., stepping on hot sand at the beach, after running around at recess, getting into a car that's been sitting in the hot sun. Have them create a simile from that experience using *like* or *as* (*as hot as burning sand at the beach; hot as a car that's been sitting in the sun*).

See page 52 for the Similes (Primary) template for use with younger students. This template originally appeared in *Writing Power*.

- Explain that there are some similes that are very common—"busy as a bee" and "wise as an owl"—but that poets don't often use them in their poems because poets are always trying to say something in a new way. Pass out the Simile and You Will See! template on page 51 for students to use to come up with new similes.
- Remind students that, when they are writing similes, both the topic and what they are comparing it to need to match. For example, saying "as hot as a chair" wouldn't really make sense because chairs aren't always hot.

Grade 4

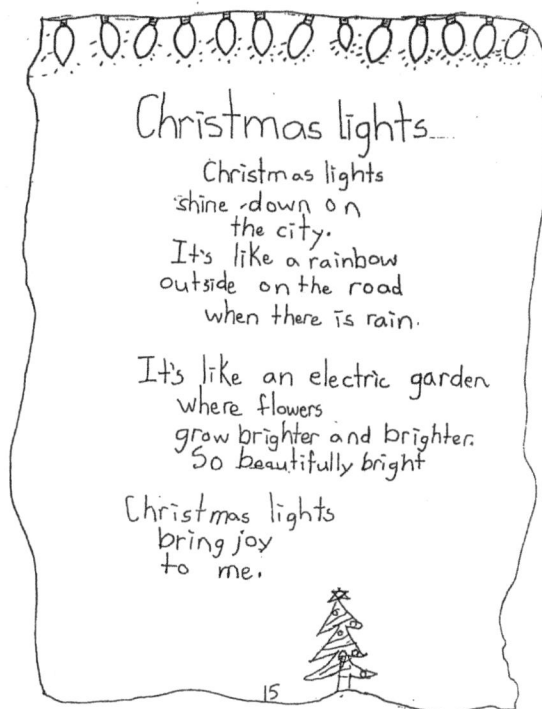

Metaphor

Teaching students about similes first can help scaffold their understanding of metaphors.

Like simile, metaphor is a figure of speech that is used to make a comparison between two things that aren't alike but do have something in common. Metaphors can create an even stronger image through a statement rather than a suggestion; e.g., a girl's cheeks aren't just *like* a shiny apple, they *are* a shiny apple. I like to think of similes as a more casual version of metaphors. Metaphors help writers and poets make a point in a more interesting way and can help the reader see something from a new perspective.

ANCHOR POEMS FOR TEACHING METAPHOR

"Friends" by Abbie Farwell Brown
"Earth Head" by Ralph Fletcher
"White Sheep, White Sheep" by Christina Rossetti

LESSON

• Begin the lesson:

  Poets, today we are going to learn a poetry technique that will help you say something old in a new way.

• Write examples of metaphors on the board.

  Her cheeks are polished apples.
  The snow is a white blanket.
  Her tears were a salty river flowing down her cheeks.

- Ask students what they notice about the sentences. (If you have taught similes, many will make a connection with them.)
- Explain that poets sometimes use this technique to make their writing more interesting by giving it a different perspective. If your students already know about similes (see page 37), you can explain that metaphors are closely related, but don't use the word *like* or *as*. I like to tell the students that metaphors are more grown-up or sophisticated (i.e., stronger, more confident) than similes because the poet is making a statement that something *is* something else, rather than *like* something else.
- Create a T-chart with the words *Metaphor* and *Simile* at the top of each column. Show the different versions of the statement. You can invite students to help you change the metaphors into similes, or similes into metaphors using the Metaphor Match chart on page 53.

SAMPLE METAPHOR/SIMILE CHART

Metaphor	Simile
Her cheeks are polished apples.	Her cheeks are shiny like a polished apple.
The snow is a white blanket.	The snow covered the grass like a white blanket.
Her tears were a salty river flowing down her cheeks.	Her tears ran down her cheeks like a salty river.

- Copy and share one of the examples of metaphor poems. I often use Christina Rosetti's "White Sheep, White Sheep" when I introduce metaphors because the comparison of a single cloud to a sheep is one most students can conceptualize. It's also easy to find on the internet!

  Read it aloud and invite students to identify the metaphor. Ask them why they think the poet used that particular comparison. (*clouds are fluffy like sheep; they move together like clouds; the blue hill is the sky*)
- Practice creating metaphors with the students. Invite them to try to help you complete the following prompts:

  My legs were _____ as I raced for the finish line. (*tornados, torpedoes*)

  Books are _____. (*friends, doors, trains*)

  My heart was a _____ when my fish died. (*heavy rock, black hole*)

  His heart was a _____ as he entered the haunted house. (*hummingbird, time bomb*)

- Share other recommended poems and invite students to identify the metaphor in them. Discuss how the metaphor helps you understand the poem in a different way.

Personification

Personification is a commonly used poetic device by which animals, plants, and inanimate objects are given human qualities. Its use results in a poem full of imagery and description. While sometimes used in prose, personification is more often associated with poetry. While the concept of transferring human characteristics to inanimate objects sounds rather sophisticated for students, once they understand and start to identify examples of personification in poetry, even young writers can begin to experiment with using it in their poems.

ANCHOR POEMS FOR TEACHING PERSONIFICATION

"April Rain Song" by Langston Hughes
"A Book" by Myra Cohn Livingston
"Whispers" by Myra Cohn Livingston
"Take a Poem to Lunch" by Denise Rogers
"Red Sings from Treetops" by Joyce Sidman
"Whatifs" by Shel Silverstein
"Snow Kisses" by Barbara Vance
"I Wandered, Lonely as a Cloud" by William Wordsworth

Anchor Books for Personification

Livingston, Myra Cohn. *Calendar*
Sidman, Joyce. *Red Sings from Treetops*

Spinelli, Eileen. *Here Comes the Year*

LESSON

- Write the word *personification* on the board. Explain that students will be learning a poetry technique called personification. Tell them it's something poets do to "add some pizazz" to their poems.
- Ask students to identify any smaller words within the word on the board that might help them figure out the meaning. (many will find small words like: *cat, at, son, if,* and *on*) Underline or circle the word *person*. Explain that the word *person* is a good way to remember what this technique is.

  Poets, personification *is when a poet writes about an object or animal as if it was a person by adding human qualities to it. What do you think "human qualities" might be? What makes a human different from this chair, for example? (move-ment/action, feelings, thoughts, voice) When a poet adds voice, movement, feel-ings, or thoughts to an object, it helps them say something old in a new way.*

- Share a few examples (see below) and discuss how personification helps the poet say something old in a new way.

  Instead of "The flowers were dry and needed water," you could write *The flowers begged for water.* (flowers can't beg)

  Instead of "The sky lit up with lightning" you could write, *Lightning danced across the sky.* (lightning can't dance)

  Instead of "The warm sun was shining," you could write *The sun greeted me with a warm smile.* (the sun doesn't smile)

Instead of "The vines grew around the tree trunk," you could write *The vines wove their thin fingers around the tree trunk.* (vines don't weave)

- Choose one of the suggested anchor poems and share it with students. Invite them to identify the poet's use of personification in the poem.
- Invite students to practice creating personification sentences. Invite them to fold a paper in half along the length, or they could make a T-chart or use the Personification Match template on page 54.
- Model on chart paper how to list inanimate objects on the left side (objects in nature work best: e.g., *leaf, snowflake, mountain, cloud, raindrop, river, tree*, etc.
- On the right side, model how students can list action words (verbs). They can describe anything a human can do with their hands (*clap, wave, tickle*, etc.), feet (*stomp, tiptoe, kick*, etc.), and mouth (*whisper, hum, kiss*, etc.).
- When both sides of the chart are complete, model how to match one word from the left side of the chart with any word on the right side. Encourage students to create unique images, avoiding ones that they may already have heard before: e.g., *the leaves danced* is common but *the leaves tickled* is new.
- Remind students that it is better to come up with a few really unique matches than to try to find a match for every word.
- Invite students to share some of their best matches. They can expand them into a sentence by adding an adverb (to indicate how) and a noun (to indicate where). Example: *snowflake tiptoes* becomes *The snowflake tiptoes softly across my cheek.*

Object in Nature	Actions of your hands, feet, or mouth
leaf	clap
snowflake	tickle
tree	tiptoe
cloud	stomp
river	whisper
raindrop	hum
mountain	giggle

Grade 4

Leaves

Leaves fall from a tree,
Dancing as they fall,
Dressed in beautiful colours.

When they get to the ground,
They sing a song
When you step on them
Crunch, crunch, crunch.

Repetition

Repetition is likely the most common and widely recognized technique poets use in their poems. Poets often repeat sounds, words, ideas, lines, or even entire stanzas. A poem might start each line with the same words, or it might repeat a stanza several times like a chorus in a song. Repetition is one device that, once students understand how simple it can be to create poetic sound, is easily used in their own poems.

ANCHOR POEMS FOR TEACHING REPETITION

"This Tooth" by Lee Bennett Hopkins
"Whispers" by Myra Cohn Livingston
"White Sheep, White Sheep" by Christina Rossetti
"Hug-O-War" by Dr. Seuss
"Skippety Stones" by Amy Ludwig VanDerwater

ANCHOR BOOKS FOR REPETITION

Frost, Robert. *Stopping By Woods on A Snowy Evening* (illustrated)

Riley, A.K. *Snow Song*
Seuss, Dr. *Green Eggs and Ham* (or any of his books)

- Begin the lesson:

  Today, poets, we are going to learn about one of the 3 R's— repetition. Just as readers enjoy rhythm and rhyme in poems, we can also find repetition enjoyable. The word repetition *comes from the word* repeat. *Who can tell me what that word means?* (to say something more than once). *Poets sometimes repeat words or phrases in their poems to help draw the reader's attention to a thought, idea, or feeling. Repetition can also make the main idea of the poem more interesting or memorable.*

- Share one of the suggested anchor poems. Read it aloud and invite students to listen for repeating words or phrases.
- Discuss which words are repeated and ask the students why they feel those words are the ones the poet used to repeat. (*to emphasize the meaning*)
- Create a class poem together using repetition. Invite students to help you write it. Start with a simple topic, like My Dog. Tell students you are going to write a poem about your dog and will be using repetition.

  My Dog

  My dog
  My dog
  I love my dog.
  Her fur is brown
  Her ears are velvet triangles
  Her tail is a fluffy feather
  Her paws smell like the forest.
  I love my dog.
  My dog
  My dog.

- Discuss the repeating words and phrases, and why you chose those words to repeat. Discuss alliteration (*fluffy feather*) and similes (*paws smell like the forest*) if you have already taught them. Remind students that using repetition can turn your ideas into a poem very easily.
- Invite students to try to write a simple repeating poem.

STUDENT SAMPLE POEMS: REPETITION

Bubble Gum by Jessie

Bubble gum
Bubble gum
Juicy pink bubble gum!
Soft, pink bubble gum!
Chewy, gooey bubble gum.
Chew it up soft
Up and down teeth.
Blow that bubble gum
Big pink bubble gum
Bigger, bigger bubble gum
POP!

The Beach

I see
The oshun
I See
See shls
I See
The sand
I See
Seegls
I See Evrying

Sun

Sun, Sun
Plaes come out,
I wont to Play with you.

Sun, Sun
Plaes come out,
My bruther wonts to see you.

Sun, Sun
You make the flowers haPPy,
And make them gerow.

Sun, Sun
You make urth warm.

Sun, Sun.
You are my frined.

Alliteration

Alliteration is a literary device of the repetition of initial consonant sounds in two or more nearby words. Alliteration does not refer to the repetition of initial letters, but rather the repetition of initial sounds. For example, "phenomenal friendship" is an example of alliteration; the initial letters are different, but they produce the same sounds; "phony people" is not an example of alliteration because, even though the two words begin with the same letter, the *p* does do not sound the same in the two words. In addition, for alliteration to be effective, alliterative words should be close together. If there are too many non-alliterative words in between, then the literary device loses its affect.

The most common form of alliteration that children may be already familiar with is tongue twisters, as the repeated sound at the beginning of several consecutive words is obvious.

ANCHOR POEMS FOR TEACHING ALLITERATION

Any tongue twister
"This Tooth" by Lee Bennett Hopkins
"Bear in There" by Shel Silverstein
"Overnight" by Amy Ludwig VanDerwater
"Rose Seller" by Amy Ludwig VanDerwater
"Soap Hope" by Amy Ludwig VanDerwater

LESSON

• Copy the following tongue twister on a chart stand or whiteboard:

Peter Piper picked a peck of pickled peppers. A peck of pickled peppers did Peter Piper pick.

- Invite students to read the sentences or read them aloud. (Many will be familiar with this tongue twister.) Invite students to say it out loud quickly.
- Tell students that this kind of verse is called a tongue twister. Ask them to share any others they may know (*She sells sea shells… How much wood could a woodchuck chuck…Rubber baby buggy bumpers*)
- Ask students what they notice about the tongue twister. (many words start with the same letter/sound) Explain that tongue twisters are examples of a poetic technique called *alliteration*—when the poet uses several words close together that begin with the same sound. Explain that poets use this technique to create a pleasing effect for readers, especially when the poem is being read out loud.
- Tell students that alliteration is often used in everyday life, in movies, and in popular culture, because it makes phrases "catchy" and easy to remember. Create a chart with some or all of the headings shown below. Depending on the grade you teach, students can help you add ideas to the chart. It's especially fun for them to "invent" new alliteration ideas to add, such as ice cream flavors.
- Share one of the recommended anchor poems. I suggest copying it out or projecting it so that students can read along and clearly identify where the alliteration is being applied.

SAMPLE ALLITERATION CHART

Everyday Alliteration	Alliteration in character names	Alliteration in pop culture	Ice Cream Flavors
big business	Lois Lane	Tik-Tok	Rocky Road
jumping jacks	Peter Parker	Candy Crush	Misty Mint
no nonsense	Wonder Woman	Hula Hoop	Peanut Butter
quick question	Miss Muffet	Coca Cola	Paradise
money matters	Bob the Builder	Dunkin' Donuts	Caramel Crunch
picture perfect	Wicked Witch of the West	Polly Pocket	Strawberry Shortcake
	Mickey Mouse	Tonka Toys	Tiger Tail
	Minnie Mouse	Teletubbies	
	Bugs Bunny	Rainbow Room	
	Daffy Duck	Fantastic Four	
	Donald Duck	Hip Hop	
	Daisy Duck	Paw Patrol	
	Pig Pen	Door Dash	
	Peppa Pig	Pretty in Pink	
	Holly Hobbie		
	Kris Kringle		

- Invite students to practice some alliterative sentences using the All About Alliteration template on page 55. Have them choose a letter they are going to focus on and create an alliterative name first (e.g., S, Silly Sam). Once they have a name, they can add an action and a location (e.g., *Silly Sam is swimming in the sea*).
- Model a few sentences and invite students to help you develop them. Remember that the sentence needs to make sense!

Careful Katie is counting carrots in her colorful garden.

Bashful Billy bats the ball before bolting to first base.

Talented Tim…

- Another option for practicing alliteration is to invite students to write a Counting on Alliteration poem. Students write a counting poem, focusing on the initial sound of each number from one to ten:

One warty witch wandering in the wilderness.
Two tiny toads tiptoeing on a toadstool.
Three thoughtful thinkers in a thunderstorm.
Four fine fish flashing their fins.
Five…
Six…

Onomatopoeia

Kenn Nesbitt has a wonderful list of rhyming onomatopoeia words that you can share with your students, if you want to challenge them to create a rhyming poem using sound words. https://www.poetry4kids.com/lessons/list-of-rhyming-onomatopoeia/

Onomatopoeia is when a word replaces and actually mimics the sound of the object or action it refers to when it is spoken; e.g., "meow," "ring, ring," "achoo," "whoosh." Onomatopoeia appeals to the sense of hearing, and poets often use this technique to bring their poem to life in the reader's head, making the description more expressive and interesting. The most common form of onomatopoeia children might be familiar with are the flash of sound words from comics and cartoons—"Bam!" "Pow!" "Splat!"

ANCHOR POEMS FOR TEACHING ONOMATOPOEIA

"Baa, Baa, Black Sheep" (traditional nursery rhyme)
"Horsey, Horsey" (traditional nursery rhyme)
"Weather is Full of the Nicest Sounds" by Aileen Fisher
"On the Ning Nang Nong" by Spike Milligan
"Swish Went the Fish" by Kelly Roper
"The Rollercoaster" by Kelly Roper
"The Fourth" by Shel Silverstein

ANCHOR BOOKS FOR ONOMATOPOEIA

Bennett, Jill. *Noisy Poems*   Heidbreder, Robert. *Noisy Poems for a Busy Day*

LESSON

It's not often I come across a word with six syllables, so I like to take a few moments to have the students clap out the syllables and practice saying the word with the correct pronunciation: *ON+UH+MAT+UH+PEE+UH*. If you teach Grade 2, prepare yourself for giggles when you say "pee"!

- Copy one of the recommended anchor poems on a chart stand or whiteboard.
- Tell students that the writer of this poem is using a special poetry technique called *onomatopoeia* (pronounced "on-uh-mat-uh-pee-uh").
- Read the poem and ask students if they notice anything special or different that the poet is using. (*sounds*)
- Explain that sound words in poems help the poet create the sensation of a sound rather than a description of the object.
- Invite students to identify examples of sound words in the poem.
- Give some examples of onomatopoeia. For example, rather than writing "the baby cried," a poet might simply write the word *Waah!* Explain that there are hundreds of words that can be used to replace a description of a sound. Invite the students to think of sound words for the following descriptions:

The wind blowing (*whoosh*)

A bell ringing (*ding-dong*)

A car braking suddenly (*screech*)

A rock dropping in the water (*plop, splash*)

- Create a sound words chart or use the Sound Words template on page 56. Begin brainstorming a few sound words for each column. Depending on the grade, you could complete this chart as a class or divide the students into small groups or pairs to work on one of the categories. Nouns can be provided, or students can think of them on their own.

Sample Sound Words Chart

Sounds Animals Make	Sounds Weather Makes	Sounds people Make	Sounds things make
horse — *neigh*	rain — *drip, splash, pitter-patter*	telling someone to be quiet — *Shhhhh*	car — *screech, vroom, beep beep!*
pig — *oink*			
frog —	hail — *crash*	crying — *Waaah!*	fire —
bee —	thunder — *Boom! Crash!*	laughing — *Ha Ha!*	phone —
owl —	snow —	snoring — *Zzzzz*	bell —
sheep —	wind —	sneezing — *Ah-choo!*	train —
crickets —	fire —	eating —	soda pop —
birds —	trees —	drinking —	ice cubes —
lion —	leaves —	singing —	pots and pans —
monkey —	ocean —	walking —	vacuum cleaner —
		fighting —	video game —

- Return to the first poem you shared or share a new poem from the list of anchor poems. Discuss how the poet uses sound words to help readers "hear" the poem, as well as see it.

STUDENT SAMPLE POEM: ONOMATOPOEIA

Grade 6

FIReWORKS!

Kaboom!
Pow!
Wow!
Colourful lights in the sky.
Screech!
Whoah!
Cool!
Those lights can fly high.
phzzzzzzz!
Skreeeeee!
Bang!
Pop! pop! pop! pop!
Oh My gosh! Such a beautiful sight.
Sighhhhh!
Swooshhh!
Booooom!
Crakle!
Pop! fizzzzzz
Pop!
So much magic in the sky.

Rhyming Patterns

Rhyme, one of the 3 R's, is a poetic device featured in some poems. Rhyming is when identical or similar concluding syllables in different words are repeated. Rhyme most often occurs at the ends of lines, and focuses more on matching sounds (aural rhyme) than spelling (visual rhyme). For example: *day*, *prey*, *weigh*, and *bouquet* have different spelling patterns, but they rhyme. Poets use rhymes as a way to create sound patterns in order to emphasize certain words and to enhance the rhythm and cadence of their poem.

There are a wide range of rhyming patterns, ranging in difficulty from the very simple ABAB pattern (where every second line of the poem rhymes) to the very complex pattern of ABAB CDCD EFEF GG that you might find in a Shakespearean sonnet.

While I'm not expecting students to memorize or master different rhyming patterns, becoming familiar with rhyme as a feature of poetry is important. One of the benchmarks of reading readiness is a child's ability to identify rhyming words. From a very early age, many children are exposed to rhyming patterns in Mother Goose and other nursery rhymes. Nursery rhymes serve as a foundation for language acquisition, reading, and listening comprehension for children, and to introduce young children to word play and rhythm.

"If a child knows 8 Nursery Rhymes by heart by the time they are 4 years old, they are usually among the best readers and spellers in their class by the time they are 8." — Mem Fox, *Reading Magic*

Don't Poems Have to Rhyme?

When it comes to teaching rhyme to students, my primary goal is to help them learn to identify rhyming words and patterns in poems that we read together orally. Writing rhyming poetry is an art, and not something that always comes naturally to children. Often, meaning and quality is sacrificed for the sake of a rhyme. Emerging and beginning writers often end up replacing powerful words with weak ones just because they rhyme, resulting in poems that sound boring and contrived. Sometimes rhyming happens by accident and works. But more often than not, I don't make rhyming a priority when my students are writing poems. That being said, there is much value in introducing and identifying rhyming words and patterns, and no harm in inviting students to experiment with it.

LESSON

- Copy "Springtime" and "Twinkle Twinkle, Little Star" onto the board or chart stand.

Springtime	Twinkle, Twinkle
The sky above is clear,	Twinkle, twinkle, little star
I hear the robins singing.	How I wonder what you are
The wind is blowing near,	Up above the world so high
I hear the chime bells ringing!	Like a diamond in the sky.

- Read aloud or invite a student to read aloud each poem.
- Ask students if they recognize either of the short poems (most will know "Twinkle, Twinkle"). Tell them that these are rhymes they might have learned in pre-school or Kindergarten. Ask if anyone remembers any other nursery rhymes ("Mary Had a Little Lamb," "Hey, Diddle Diddle," "Jack and Jill," etc.)

- Discuss the 3 R's of the two poems on the chart. Neither have repetition, but the rhyming words are what classifies them as short poems.
- Explain that not all poems rhyme, but the ones that do rhyme use different rhyming patterns. Explain that a rhyming pattern tells us which lines of the poem rhyme with other lines. Tell them that there are many different rhyming patterns used in poetry. The important thing is, once you start using a rhyming pattern in your poem, you can't switch to another one.
- Ask students to identify the rhyming words in each poem (*clear–near, singing—ringing; star–are, high–sky*) Underline the rhyming words using different colors. Discuss how "Springtime" has a rhyming pattern where every second line rhymes, while in "Twinkle, Twinkle," the first two lines rhyme and the next two rhyme.
- Write AABB and ABAB on the board. Explain that these are both codes for different rhyming patterns. Ask students which rhyming patten they think matches each poem.
- Write the codes at the end of the each line of the poem. (see below)

SAMPLE RHYMING PATTERN IDENTIFICATION

Springtime	**Twinkle, Twinkle**
The sky above is clear, **A**	Twinkle, twinkle, little star **A**
I hear the robins singing. **B**	How I wonder what you are **A**
The wind is blowing near, **A**	Up above the world so high **B**
I hear the chime bells ringing! **B**	Like a diamond in the sky. **B**

- For the next few days, practice identifying rhyming patterns in different poems or nursery rhymes. Depending on your grade level, choose a few more complex patterns, such as AABBC.
 The Rhyme Time practice template on page 57 can be used for independent practice or with the whole class.

Simile and You Will See!

Name: _____

	Familiar	Original
As cold as…	*ice*	*the monkey bars in winter.*
Hot like …	the sun	
As brave as…	a lion	
As slow as…	a turtle	
As white as…	snow	
As quiet as…	a mouse	
As black as…	night	
As funny as…	a clown	
As annoying as…	a mosquito	
As boring as…	watching paint dry	
As busy as…	a bee	
Soft like…	a kitten	
As wise as…	an owl	
Quick as…	a bunny	

Pembroke Publishers © 2021 *Powerful Poetry* by Adrienne Gear ISBN 978-1-55138-352-1

Similes (Primary)

Name: _____

As big as…	
As white as…	
As shiny as…	
Small like a…	
As funny as a…	
Quiet like a…	
Slow like a…	
As fast as a…	

Metaphor Match

Name: _____

Turn each simile into a metaphor. Try making your own pair in the last two rows.

Simile	Metaphor
Her heart pounded like a drum.	Her heart was a pounding drum.
They danced like a graceful swan.	They were a graceful swan dancing across the stage.
The wind was gentle, like a butterfly.	
Your face is as white as a sheet.	
His hands are cold, like ice cubes.	
Her heart soared like an eagle.	
Her brain was like a computer filled with files.	
He ran as fast as a cheetah.	

Pembroke Publishers © 2021 *Powerful Poetry* by Adrienne Gear ISBN 978-1-55138-352-1

Personification Match

Name: _____

Object in Nature	Action Word (something you can do with your hands, feet, or mouth)

All About Alliteration

Name: _____

Choose a letter:

Create a two-word character name with each word starting with the same sound (example: Careful Kate)

_____

Brainstorm things that begin with the same sound.

Objects	Places
_____	_____
_____	_____
_____	_____
_____	_____
_____	_____

Write *who-what-where* alliteration sentences about your character: for example, *Careful Kate counts carrots in her colorful garden.*

_____

_____

_____

Sound Words

Name: _____

Sounds Animals Make	Sounds Nature Makes	Sounds People Make	Sounds Things Make
horse — *neigh*	rain — *drip, splash, pitter-patter*	telling someone to be quiet —	car — *honk! honk!*
pig –	hail –	*Shhhhh*	fire engine –
frog –	thunder –	crying –	phone –
bee –	snow –	laughing –	bell –
owl –	wind –	snoring –	train –
sheep –	fire –	sneezing –	soda pop –
crickets –	trees –	eating –	ice cubes –
birds –	leaves –	drinking –	pots and pans –
lion –	ocean —	singing –	vacuum cleaner –
monkey —		walking –	video game —
		fighting —	

Rhyme Time

Name: _____

Read each poem. Underline the last word in each line. Look for the rhyming pattern. Record the pattern: **AABB**, **ABAB**, or **ABCB**.

Mrs. Brown and the Fancy Gown	**What a Day!**
Mrs. Brown had a fancy gown But sadly wore it upside down. The neckline round her toes And the frills tickled her nose.	I started playing baseball But my bat ran out of swing. I started singing opera But my voice ran out of sing.
Rhyme pattern: _____	**Rhyme Pattern**: _____
My Brain Has Stopped	**I Had an Epic Day**
My brain has stopped, My eyes are blurry, My ears have popped, It's time to worry!	Today I had an epic day! As I was coming in from play, I met a superhero guy Who kindly taught me how to fly!
Rhyme Pattern: _____	**Rhyme Pattern**: _____

Now it's your turn! Try to write a 4-line poem for each of the rhyming patterns. Remember—your poem has to make sense!

I like my cat   A

_____ A

_____ B

_____ B

Play in the sun   A

_____ B

_____ A

_____ B

Poetic Structures

"I'm sort of annoyed that some very basic things about poetic forms were not conveyed to me in the various poetry courses I took over the years." — Juliana Spahr

The inner structure of every poem—the frame, the number of lines, the stanzas, the rhyming pattern, the length—is what holds it together. In my book *Powerful Writing Structures*, I outline the different structures of writing introduced in elementary school: personal narrative, nonfiction writing, story writing, and poetry. Just as *nonfiction* is a broad term under which there are many different structures (persuasion, description, instruction, etc.), so, too, does poetry include a range of different structures.

These are the most common poetic structures introduced in elementary school:

Haiku: 3 lines, 5-7-5 syllable pattern, usually about nature.
Cinquain: 5 lines, 2-4-6-8-2 syllables
Acrostic: the first letter of each line spells a word
List Poem: describes a topic by creating a list
Concrete: combination of poetry and art; the poem takes the shape of its subject
Found Poem: uses words from a previously written text
Free verse: doesn't rhyme or have a set number of syllables.
Limerick: a short, silly rhyming poem with an AABBA rhyme scheme

"Poetry is the most mistaught subject in any school because we teach poetry by form and not by content." — Nikki Giovanni

Form Over Art?

These forms are likely not new to anyone. We all learned them in high-school English classes or elementary school. There are literally hundreds of Poetry Units available on Pinterest, Teachers Pay Teachers, and online, and most, if not all, include lessons on different poetic structures. Teachers introduce haiku poetry, for example: students learn the 5-7-5 count; they may or may not learn the Japanese origin and the focus on nature; they follow the structure and create a haiku poem that follows the 5-7-5 structure:

My cat is furry.
My cat likes to play with me.
I love my cute cat.

Is this a haiku poem? One could argue it is because it follows the structure, and mastering the 5-7-5 syllable count is no easy task, especially for younger writers. So there is much to celebrate with this cat haiku. But is structure enough? Is this poem saying something old in a new way? Is it poetic?

One of the dangers of teaching poetry through structure alone is that most poems children write from this approach lack any semblance of poetry. Poetic structure alone does not create a poem; a poem is greater than the sum of its parts. A poet might use the structure as their foundation, but from it emerges something magical: an image, a feeling, a surprise—sprinkled with a few literary techniques.

And so, while we must provide lessons in poetic structure when teaching poetry, unless we combine them with lessons on what poetry is, unless we teach

It's important to note that one of the common features of every poetic structure is that it can be about anything, making it easy to connect any of these structures to content areas.

poetic devices, and, above all, unless we immerse our students in the joy of poems, poetic structure becomes meaningless. No matter what poetic structure or tools we teach our students, we need to always remember that the goal of teaching poetry is to imprint it on our students' hearts and help them discover the poems hidden inside them. So, while I am about to provide lessons on eight different poetic structures, I caution you: it is only in combination with the preceding lessons that these structures will create true poetry.

Haiku

Anchor Poem for Teaching Haiku

"Old Pond" by Matsuo Basho (note that the English translation does not follow the 5-7-5 syllable count)

Features of Haiku

- a form of poetry originating in Japan
- made famous by Japanese poet Matsuo Basho
- consists of 3 lines, each with a specific syllable count: 5-7-5
- usually about nature
- often says something old in a new way
- leaves the reader with a feeling, a visual image, or a surprise
- usually includes a poetic device

ANCHOR BOOKS FOR HAIKU

Clements, Andrew. *DogKu*
Mannis, Celeste. *One Leaf Rides the Wind*
Muth, Jon J. *Hi, Koo: A Year of Seasons*
O'Connell George, Kristine. *Fold Me A Poem*

Paul, Miranda. *Thanku: Poems of Gratitude*
Raczka, Bob. *Guyku: A Year of Haiku for Boys*
Snyder, Betsy. *I Haiku You*

A mistake often made when teaching haiku is assuming that each line needs to be a separate sentence. If you look closely at the examples of published haikus, the first two lines often make up a single sentence.

The structure of a haiku is a relatively simple one for students to understand. Once they know how to count syllables, it can become a simple matter of finding a word that fits the count. One of the mistakes I see when teaching haiku, however, is when the syllable count becomes more important than the poem itself. Effective haiku poems are much more than a syllable count. They capture a single moment in nature; with only a few words, they paint a picture and often surprise us.

Before having your students write their own haiku, share as many haiku poems as you can with them (see recommended books). Immerse students in the form! Haiku are short so they are easy to copy out on chart paper or a shared screen. Read them out loud, notice, and discuss:

> *What is this haiku about?*
> *What are you noticing?*
> *What do you feel?*
> *What are you visualizing?*
> *What poetic devices did the poet use?*
> *How did the poet say something old in a new way?*

- Copy this haiku on the board:

  My cat is fluffy
  My cat likes to play with me.
  I love my cute cat.

- Read the haiku and ask students what they think of it. (*It's a little boring!*) Does it have the 5-7-5 count? (*yes*) Does the poem flow smoothly? (*sounds a bit choppy*) Does the poem say something old in a new way? (*no*)
- Explain that, for haiku (pronounces "high-koo"), the 5-7-5 syllable count is the frame. But equally important as the syllable count, is that the poem should leave the reader with a feeling, a visual image, or a little surprise.
- Explain that one way to write haiku is to start with the ideas, not the syllables. Another way to help the haiku flow is by writing one longer and one shorter sentence rather than three choppy ones.
- Tell students you will be sharing some secrets for writing the perfect haiku poem! Model the following steps to create a class haiku:

  Step 1: Choose a topic in nature (e.g., the wind).

  Step 2: Write a sentence describing, in detail, what the wind does. Try to include a feeling:
  The wind blows the leaves all over my yard after I finish raking them into a pile. It's frustrating.

  Step 3: Now, try to say that in a new way, maybe using personification or a simile:
  Just when I think I'm finished raking, the wind changes its mind and I have to start all over again!

  Step 4: Now, work on the syllables: 5-7-5. Don't worry about a new idea for each line:
  When I think I am
  Finished raking the leaves, the
  Wind decides I'm not.

- Ask students what poetic device you used (*personification: the wind "decides"*). Ask students if the poem says something old in a new way. (*"Wind decides I'm not" instead of saying "the wind blew the leaves after I raked"*)
- Pass out the Let's Write Haiku! template on page 84 and invite students to try to follow the steps to practice writing their own haiku.

EXTENSION

Challenge students to write several haiku based on a theme:

Seasons: one haiku for each season (fall, winter, spring, summer)
Sports: one haiku for each different sport (basketball, baseball, hockey, lacrosse)
Pets: several haiku about different pets (dogs, cats, fish, hamsters)
Habitats: forest, desert, arctic, grassland

Grade 2

Fall
Nuts Playing minigolf
The rake plays tag with the leaves
it must be Fall. Yeah!

BY PAtricio

Grade 3

Bee

flying so quickly
over beautiful flowers
Yellow, black airplane

by Alan

Cinquain Poetry

While I have not yet found a whole poetry book that features only cinquains, children's poet Kenn Nesbitt has some excellent examples of cinquain poetry on his website: www.poetry4kids.com

Cinquain is another popular form of poetry to teach students. It was created by American poet Adelaide Crapsey about 100 years ago. It is similar to Japanese poetic forms, such as haiku and tanka, because its simple structure is based on syllable count. Cinquains are only five lines long, with only a few words on each line, making them easy for students to write. The first and last lines have two syllables, while the middle lines have more, so they end up with a diamond-like shape. Like haiku, cinquain poems that focus on structure alone often end up sounding contrived and choppy. The best cinquains tell a small story. Instead of just listing describing words about a topic, they may also have actions, feelings, and an ending.

Features of Cinquain Poetry

- consists of five lines
- lines have a syllable count of 2-4-6-8-2: 2 syllables in the first line, 4 in the second, 6 in the third, 8 in the fourth line, and 2 in the last line
- can be about anything
- often tells a little story
- can include actions, feelings, and an ending
- may or may not rhyme
- can include poetic devices

- Tell your poets you are going to be showing them a new kind of poem today called a cinquain (pronounced "sin-cane").
- Explain that it is a five lined poem that, like haiku, has a specific syllable count per line—2, 4, 6, 8, 2.
- Tell students that, like haiku, the syllables are the frame, but the poem also needs to make sense and tell a little story.
- Show students an example of a cinquain. Note that the poem looks a little bit like a diamond on the page.

Kitten

She is so cute.

She has grey and white stripes.

She eats crunchy food from a bowl.

Yum yum.

- Read the poem aloud. Ask students if the poem follows the correct syllable structure (*yes*). Ask the students if it looks like a poem (*yes*). Ask if the poem says something old in a new way (*NO! It just describes facts about the kitten, doesn't sound like a poem*).
- Read the second Kitten example:

Kitten

Tiny nose, ears

like velvet triangles,

Tiny sandpaper tongue licking.

Bath time

- Ask students what they notice, what part they like best, and what makes it different from the other poem. (*Sounds more like a poem; senses, simile;, not a new sentence on every line; ending is a little surprise*)
- Tell students they are going to try to write their own cinquain:

    Poets, you can learn to write cinquains by following these simple steps:
    - *Decide what you would like to write about. (You can write about anything!)*
    - *Brainstorm words and phrases that have to do with your idea.*
    - *Think about what story you want to tell.*
    - *Write your words and phrases in an order that tells your story, being sure to count the syllables as you go.*

For more on the Memory Pocket and Brain Pocket writing, see chapter 4.

- Model writing a cinquain in front of the class, doing a write-aloud.

    First, you need to select a topic for your cinquain. Let's try using our Memory Pocket to find a topic. You could write about your favorite thing, something you don't like, something you see around you, something you like to do.

    Since reading is my favorite thing, I think I'll write a cinquain about reading. This is convenient since the word "reading" has two syllables, so I can probably use this word as the first line of my cinquain. It helps if your favorite thing has two syllable— like pizza, soccer, *or* ice cream, *because then you can use that as your first line.*

- Explain that, once you know what your poem is going to be about, the next thing is to brainstorm ideas *about* your topic. Think of as many things as you can and write them down. Remind them not to worry about syllables at this point.

> READING
> - brings me joy
> - a great escape
> - you don't need batteries
> - books smell good

- Explain that these are four ideas, but they are not yet a poem. To turn these ideas into a cinquain poem, you need to arrange them in five lines with the right number of syllables on each line and tell a little story.
- Model using your fingers to do a syllable count. Make changes as you find different words to fit the syllables. Ask students to help you think of words for your poem.
- Remind them that syllables are important, but that the poem needs to make sense and tell a little story.

Reading

Reading.
The great escape.
I love the smell of books.
No batteries required for
book joy.

- Discuss what they notice about your poem. (*It tells a little story; there is an action*—smelling books; *there is a little surprise*—no batteries required; *and a feeling*—book joy.)
- Pass out the Let's Write a Cinquain template on page 85. Review the steps: Think of a topic; brainstorm the topic; write your poem.
- If students struggle when it comes to taking their brainstorm list and turning it into a poem, tell them that sometimes it helps to think of each line telling something different:

Line 1: topic (2 syllables)

Line 2: description (4 syllables)

Line 3: action (6 syllables)

Line 4: feeling (8 syllables)

Line 5: ending (2 syllables)

Diamante

A diamante, or diamond poem, is a seven-lined poem created in 1969 by an American poet named Iris McClellan Tiedt. Because of its diamond shape, Tiedt named the poetic form *diamante*, the Italian word for diamond. The first and last lines are the shortest, while the lines in the middle are progressively longer and then shorter, giving it a diamond shape. Over the years, it has become a very popular poetic form in schools because of its simple-to-follow structure and the fact that you can throw in a grammar lesson on parts of a sentence at the same time! It is also a poetic structure that can be effectively integrated into Social Studies, Science and other curriculum areas; see Comparing Poems on page 123.

There are two different types of diamantes: *synonym* and *antonym*. In a synonym diamante, the first and last word in the poem mean the same; in an antonym diamante, the first and last words are opposites. Synonym diamantes are slightly easier, so for the purpose of the lesson, I will be focusing on this type. For those who prefer the antonym alternative, there is information about the antonym diamante at the end of the lesson.

Features of a Diamante Poem

- shaped like a diamond
- 7 lines long
- does not rhyme
- combines nouns, adjectives, and verbs
- has a strict structure based on word count and parts of speech:

    Lines 1 and 7: 1 word (noun)
    Lines 2 and 6: 2 words (adjectives)
    Lines 3 and 5: 3 words (verbs)
    Line 4: 4 words (nouns)

ANCHOR BOOKS FOR DIAMANTE

I have yet to find an entire poetry book devoted to diamante poetry, but you can find many examples on the internet and in books about teaching poetry, including

Harley, Avis. *Fly With Poetry*   Janeczko, Paul B. *Teaching 10 Fabulous Forms of Poetry*

LESSON

- Draw a diamond on the board and ask students what shape it is.
- Tell them that you are going to be showing them a new poem that is shaped like a diamond. Explain that it is actually named after the Italian word for diamond, which is diamante (pronounced "dee-uh-MAHN-tay"). Invite students to say the word aloud—with an Italian accent, of course!
- Share and show a diamante poem to students. Before reading, point out the shape of the poem.

    Explain that, to form the correct shape, the diamante poem has specific rules about how many and what kind of words are included on each line. However, they do not need to worry about syllable counting when they write a diamante.

- Copy the following on the board:

Noun	1 word
Adjective, Adjective	2 words
Verb, Verb, Verb	3 words
Noun, Noun, Noun, Noun	4 words
Verb, Verb, Verb	3 words
Adjective, Adjective	2 words
Noun	1 word

- Continue the lesson:

  As with many poems, once a poet decides on the structure, they need decide on the topic. For a diamante, your topic needs to be a noun or a thing, because your first and last lines of the poem need to be nouns. You could choose to write about a pizza, a pencil, an alien, or a ladybug. The easiest thing is to choose something you like or something you can see around you. I think I'm going to write about a book because I LOVE books!

  (Feel free to choose your own topic.)

- Write the word *Book* on the chart stand or board. It's helpful to create blank lines for words (1–2–3–4–3–2–1) in the shape of the diamante beforehand so you can simply fill in the words on the lines as you write your poem.
- Explain that the next line in the poem needs to include two adjectives or describing words. Invite students to help you think of words to describe a book. (*adventurous, thrilling, enchanting, exciting, intense, addictive, amazing, calming, fascinating, gripping, hilarious, heartbreaking*) Choose two of the adjectives and write them underneath the word *Book*.
- Tell students that the next line needs to be made up of three verbs or action words connected to a book. (*buying, opening, sniffing, reading, thinking, dreaming, escaping, collecting, holding, turning, sharing, talking, wanting, loving*) Choose three words and write them on the third line of your poem.
- Explain that line 4 is a list of four more nouns connected to your word. Invite students to think of things (nouns) connected to a book. (*library, bookshelf, pages, cover, title, chapters, beginnings, endings, adventure, mystery, illustrations, author, illustrator*) Choose four words and record them in the middle of your poem.
- Explain that the second half of the poem is going to be a little easier because you have already brainstormed a lot of verbs and adjectives. Choose from your generated list to finish your poem. You might suggest using alliteration by choosing words that begin with the same sound.

> Inspirassion.com is an amazing website that helps you find parts of speech connected to topics. A GREAT resource for writing diamantes!

Book

exciting, enchanting

reading, relaxing, escaping

cover, pages, words, chapters

buying, collecting, sharing

addictive, amazing

story

Try having students write antonym diamantes for two opposite characters in a novel. It's a great way to show different character traits.

Students who would like the challenge of the antonym diamante can use the Antonym Diamante template on page 124.

- Pass out the Diamante Poem template on page 86. Review the steps of the poem and emphasize the importance of brainstorming words before you start writing.

ANTONYM DIAMANTE LESSON

- Depending on the grade level, you might wish to introduce antonym diamantes after trying the synonym version. For an antonym diamante, the poet needs to choose two nouns that are opposite: e.g., sun–moon, pencil–eraser, dog–cat, fairy–witch, desert–rainforest, Superman–Spiderman.
- Continue the lesson:

Once you have selected your opposite words, make two columns and brainstorm as many words as you can think of for each of them. Try to include adjectives (descriptive words), verbs (action words) and more nouns connected to the word. Once you've chosen your two nouns, take a piece of paper and brainstorm as many words as you can that have to do with each of them.

SAMPLE BRAINSTORM FOR ANTONYM DIAMANTE

Fairy	Witch
Kind	Mean
Pretty	Ugly
Sparkles	Darkness
Wings	Warts
Wand	Broom
Flying	Casting spells
Magic	Destroying
Helping	Cackling

- Once the list is complete, students arrange the poem with the top of the diamante (lines 1–3) focusing on one topic and the bottom (lines 5–7) focusing on the opposite. The middle (line 4) includes two words from the top and then switches to two words from the bottom.

Fairy

pretty, kind

sparkling, flying, helping,

wand, wings, warts, broom

cackling, destroying, haunting,

ugly, mean

Witch

Acrostic Poems

The first letters of the lines of an acrostic poem typically spell a word related to the poem's topic. Because you can choose any topic for an acrostic poem, the opportunities to link to content areas are endless. Most teachers use acrostic poems as their go-to poetry lesson because it's easy to teach and easy for kids to do: Choose a topic, write the word down the side of the paper, think of a word or phrase for each letter connected to your topic—done! Let's face it, who hasn't had their students make acrostic name poems during the first week of school?

However, the simple, standard "single-scoop" format results in simple, rather boring poems. By adding a little sophistication to the style and sprinkling in a few similes, your students can create "triple-scoop" acrostic poems, sure to impress!

Features of Acrostic Poem

- the letters spelling out the topic of the poem or a related word are written down the left side of the page
- each letter is used as the first letter of a word or phrase connected to the topic
- usually the first letter of each line is capitalized to make it easier to see the word spelled out vertically down the page.
- it can be about anything
- does not need to rhyme or have rhythm

ANCHOR BOOKS FOR ACROSTIC POEMS

Cleary, Brian P. *Bow-Tie Pasta: Acrostic Poems*
Hummon, David. *Animal Acrostics*

Paolilli, Paul. *Silver Seeds*
Schnur, Steven. *Autumn: An Alphabet Acrostic*

LESSON

I recommend projecting your anchor acrostic poem onto a screen or copying it on chart paper, so students can see how the poem is written around and through the topic letters.

- Tell students that they will be learning a type of poetry called *acrostic* (some students will likely be familiar with this form). Explain that an acrostic poem uses letters from a word going down the page, and lines going across the page.
- Explain that all acrostic poems follow the same three steps:

  1. Choose a word that will be the topic for your poem.
  2. Write the word down the left side of the page.
  3. Write a word (or phrase or sentence) that starts with each letter, connected to the topic.

  Students can use the Acrostic Poem template on page 87 if they wish.
- Continue the lesson:

See *Powerful Writing Structures* for more on single-, double-, and triple-scoop words.

  Acrostic poems can be very simple or very fancy. There are "single-scoop," "double-scoop," and "triple-scoop" acrostic poems. Let's start with the single scoop!

- Write the word *WINTER* down the left side of a chart paper or the whiteboard. Invite students to help you think of a word for each letter connected to winter.

  Topic: WINTER

  White
  Ice
  Nippy
  Toboggan
  Earmuffs
  Reindeer

- Explain that this acrostic poem is single-scoop simple because, while the words are connected to the topic, they are just single words.
- Model a Double-Scoop Delight acrostic poem by adding details to each of the words to make a descriptive sentence. Invite students to help you.

> **W**hite snow falling softly.
> **I**ce covering the sidewalks.
> **N**ippy wind blows against my cheeks.
> **T**oboggans racing down the slippery slope.
> **E**armuffs covering my frosty ears.
> **R**eindeer bringing Christmas to all.

Point out that, while this poem is much more interesting than the single-scoop, each letter still connects to a separate idea. The poem is lovely but sounds a little choppy.

- Explain that a Tremendous Triple-Scoop acrostic poem uses the letters but does not stop at the end of each line with a new idea for each letter. The poem flows across the letters rather than "chopping and stopping" at each one. Sometimes, two or three letters are connected by one longer sentence or idea. Triple-scoop acrostics also include poetic devices, such as simile, personification, and alliteration. Model a triple scoop acrostic:

> **W**hite snow falls softly like a ballerina while
> **I**ce layers the sidewalks and the wind
> **N**ips against my cheek. My
> **T**oboggan races down the slippery slopes. Thankful for
> **E**armuffs. Listen! Can you hear the
> **R**eindeer bringing Christmas?

- Discuss the differences between this poem and the single-scoop acrostic poem. Invite students to identify the simile (*snow falls like a ballerina*) and the alliteration (*slippery slopes*). This version of acrostic poem is more challenging, but it can really transform this rather simplistic form into a sophisticated poem. Invite the students to use the What's the Scoop? Acrostic Poems template on page 88 to try single-, double-, and triple-scoop acrostic poems using a nonfiction topic they are learning about.

STUDENT SAMPLE POEM: DOUBLE-SCOOP ACROSTIC

Grade 4

Eyes super sharp searching from either side.
At the top of the food chain
Giant wingspan soaring threw the sky
Little rabbits, squerrils, and rodents — BEWARE!
Enemy is near!
BY Sam

List Poems

A list poem is just that—a list! List poetry is relatively easy to write because the lines are short—usually only two words per line—and because you can write a list poem on just about any topic you can imagine. List poems, like acrostic poems, are popular among teachers because there are very few rules and the structure is simple to follow. While some list poems I have included below rhyme, I often don't focus on rhyming when teaching list poetry because, as with other structures, a focus on the rhyming words can often detract from the poem's meaning. However, for those who want a little added challenge, it can be relatively simple to add a few rhymes to a list poem.

Features of a List Poem

- an inventory of people, places, actions, things, or ideas connected by a topic
- written as a list down the centre of the page
- the title often says what is being listed
- often includes three parts: a beginning, an ending, and a long list of things in the middle
- can be about anything
- sometimes rhymes

Anchor Book for List Poems

Heard, Georgia, ed. *Falling Down the Page: A Book of List Poems*

ANCHOR POEMS FOR TEACHING LIST POEMS

"What I Hate About Winter" by Douglas Florian (see also his list poems about the other seasons)

"What I Like About Winter" by Douglas Florian

"Weather is Full of the Nicest Sounds" by Mary Ann Hoberman (can also be used for teaching onomatopoeia)

"That Explains It" by Kenn Nesbitt

"Bleezer's Ice Cream" by Jack Prelutsky

"Sick" by Shel Silverstein

"To Do List" by Amy Ludwig VanDerwater

LESSON

- Project or copy any of the recommended list poems onto chart paper or project on a shared screen.
- Read the poem aloud once, then ask students to read it with you.
- Invite students to help identify any of the 3 R's (rhyme and rhythm, repetition).
- Ask students what they notice about the way the poem looks (*written down the centre of the page, short lines, middle section looks like a list*).
- Explain that this poem is called a *list poem*. A list poem focuses on a single topic and lists words connected to the topic. Topics can be anything: places (park, school, beach), sports (hockey, soccer, baseball) seasons (summer, winter, spring, fall), events (cultural celebrations, birthdays), food (candy, pizza, fruit), weather (snow, wind, storms), or anything else.

- Tell students that list poems often have a beginning and an ending, with the list coming in the middle.
- Invite students to choose a topic; e.g., school. Ask students to brainstorm things connected to the topic: *kids, classrooms, desks, office, principal, students, pencils, erasers, homework, tests, playground, lunchroom, math, library, bell,* etc. Record the words in a list.
- Explain that list poems only sometimes rhyme, but they always have some kind of rhythm or repetition. Explain that the way to create rhythm and repetition in a list poem is by using the same endings to your words; e.g.,*-ing* or *-er*.
- Invite them to think of some action words that end in *-ing* that are connected to the words on the list; e.g., *kids arriving, teacher welcoming, desk scraping, pencils scratching, homework searching.*
- Once the list of action words is complete, explain that they won't necessarily be kept in this order. Look over the list and ask students if there is a little story you could tell in the poem; e.g., begin at the start of the day and then end when the bell goes at the end of the day.
- Ask students to help you rewrite the poem in a storytelling sequence. Where possible, show how to rhyme two consecutive lines; e.g., *breaking–making, munching–crunching.*
- Once the list is complete, add the beginning and ending lines.

School

Every day I go to school.
Kids arriving
Teachers welcoming
Desks scraping
Homework searching
Pencils scratching
Library whispering
iPads breaking
Projects making
Playground climbing
Lunchroom munching
Lineup crunching
Principal announcing
Basketballs bouncing
Choir singing
School bell ringing
I'll be back tomorrow!

- Tell students that they will be writing their own list poems. Pass out the List Poem template on page 89. Review the steps:

How to write a list poem:

1. Choose a topic.
2. Brainstorm words connected to the topic.
3. Add an *-ing* action word (verb) to each word.
4. Read over the list and see if there is a story you could tell.
5. Rewrite the list poem in storytelling sequence.
6. Add a beginning and ending.

On the left: Grade 6

On the right: Grade 3

Hockey by Jeremy

It's hockey time!
Heart racing
Coaches pacing
Puck dropping
Goalie flopping
Players gliding
Puck sliding
Sticks passing
Sticks slashing
Goal scoring
Light flashing
Players hugging
Crowd cheering
Dads beering
Team winning
Fans grinning
It's playoff time!

Pet Store by Manjit

Please can I go to the Pet Store?
Kittens licking
Puppies playing
Goldfish swimming
Parrots talking
Hamsters spinning
Snakes curling
Kids begging
But mom says no.

EXTENSION

Lists work well for autobiographical poems. I sometimes teach list poems at the beginning of the year and invite students to write "two-worder" list poems about themselves.

STUDENT SAMPLE POEM: AUTOBIOGRAPHICAL LIST POEM

Korina

Loves unicorns
Plays soccer
TikTok dancer
Wants puppy
Any color
Hates broccoli
Loves ice cream
Many friends
Among Us
Favorite game

Concrete Poems

Concrete poetry, sometimes called "shape poetry" or "picture poetry," is poetry whose visual appearance matches the topic of the poem. The subject and meaning of the poem are illustrated by the words that form its shape. Shape poetry has been around since the 3rd century, when the Ancient Greeks began adding characters to their poetry in a visually pleasing way. In the 1950s, some Brazilian poets started making shape poems and branded them Concrete Poems. These were poems where the way the words looked on the page was equally as important as the meaning.

There are two different styles of concrete poetry. In Outline Poems, words of the poem "fill in" an outline shape of the topic of the poem. In Drawing Poems, lines of the poem are used to make the lines of the drawing. For the purpose of this lesson, I will be focusing on Outline Poems.

SAMPLE OUTLINE POEM	SAMPLE DRAWING POEM
"Snowman" by Kenn Nesbitt	"The Guardian," poet unknown

It's
cold outside.
I don't want to go
outdoors and play.
But mum says
I have to
anyway.
It's starting to snow
brrrr...   and I'm going to freeze -   brrrr...
I hate playing outside on days like these.
brrrr...   But wait a sec, I've had the   brrrr...
most amazing, brilliant idea!
I'll cover myself up
with snow and I'll
hide in here!

~The Guardian~

Outline vs Drawing

I am using the outline form for this lesson, rather than the drawing form. Depending on your grade level, you could give students the option to use the drawing form. Rather than filling in the shape with their words, they can write the words directly along the outline of the shape. In my experience, however, this drawing option can be physically challenging for beginning writers, as they have to print quite small, and they have to keep rotating the paper in order to write the poem along the outline.

Features of a Concrete Poem

- takes the shape of the subject
- combines poetry with visual images
- often written about an object
- has meaning and structure
- can include poetic devices

ANCHOR BOOKS FOR CONCRETE POETRY

Cleary, Brian P. *Ode to a Commode: Concrete Poems*
Graham, Joan Bransfield. *Splish Splash*

Janeczko, Paul B. *A Poke in the I: A Collection of Concrete Poems*
Raczka, Bob. *Wet Cement — A Mix of Concrete Poems*

"The Mouse's Tale" by Lewis Carroll
"Easter Wings" by George Herbert
"Snowman" by Kenn Nesbitt

LESSON

- Share several examples of concrete poetry on a screen, if possible. It's important that students see these poems so they can appreciate the shapes as well as the words.
- Read a poem and ask students what they notice (*poem is written in a shape*).
- Explain that this is a special kind of poem called *concrete* or *picture poetry*, for which the poet writes their poem in the shape of the topic of the poem. You might wish to describe the two different types of concrete poems—outline and drawing (see above)—and show examples of each.
- Tell students that the important thing about concrete poetry is that you write the poem first, before you create your picture. Concrete poems do not need to rhyme, but should include some poetic techniques, such as simile, alliteration, or personification (see lessons on pages 37–49).
- Model the steps of writing a concrete poem, doing a write-aloud and inviting students to help you.

> *Poets, the first step is to choose a topic for your concrete poem. The topic should be an object that has a simple or distinct shape you can draw, like a kite, ice cream cone, or soccer ball. I think I'm going to choose a tree because it's an easy shape to draw and also I like being in the forest with trees.*
> Write the word *Tree* on the board or chart paper.
> *The next step is to brainstorm words or ideas connected to my topic. I might not use all my words in the poem, but I want to start getting my ideas out. I want to try to use describing words like color and size, but also some features, feelings, and triple-scoop words. Who can help me?*
> Record ideas under the word tree on the chart paper.
> TREE
> Green
> Tall
> Majestic *What a great triple-scoop word!*
> Old—trunk rings tell age
> Home to many insects and animals
> Trees get cut down
> Calm
> *Now, I'm going to start writing my poem. I don't want to make it too long because it has to fit inside a shape. Remember the poem does not have to rhyme but it should sound like a poem and not just a description. I think I will use personification and write as if I were a tree.*

- Present your modeled concrete poem; poetic devices are noted

  Tree by A. Gear

  I stand majestic.
  Home to singers, stingers and sleepers (*alliteration*)
  Inside my trunk I hide my age (*saying something old in a new way*)

But don't cut me down to count.
Trust me when I tell you: I am an ancient one.
My roots are deep, my branches tall
Snow sticks,
Rain drips,
Needles glisten.
Listen (*a little rhyming*)
To my story.

- Ask students what makes this sound like a poem. What poetic devices do they notice? What feeling does it give them?
- Lightly, in pencil, draw the outline of a tree on chart paper or the board. Explain that you are going to copy the poem inside the tree shape. Tell students you are going to press lightly because this is where you find out how it's going to fit and whether you need to make your writing larger or smaller.
- Fill in the shape with the words from your poem. Model where you might need to make your writing bigger or smaller. Tell them it is okay if the poem doesn't fit into the shape the first time. They can keep erasing and redoing until they are happy with how it fits. Once you are happy with how the poem fits, explain how you would do a final copy on a new paper, starting with a very light outline of the shape.
- The last step is to erase the pencil outline of the poem so only the poem is making the shape of the topic, not the outline.
- Model the option of adding some additional sound-effect words to add another element to the picture; for example, in my poem I included *rain drips*.
- Invite students to write their own concrete poem. You might want to do a quick brainstorm of ideas and ensure students have selected topics with good shapes before passing out the Concrete Poem Planning Page on page 90.

STUDENT SAMPLES: CONCRETE POETRY

On the left: Grade 4

On the right: Grade 5

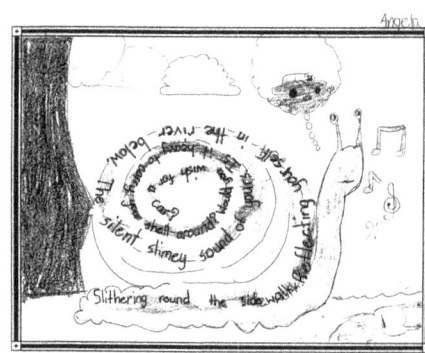

Limerick

Limericks are one of the most well-known poetic forms. Most people assume that they originated in the Irish county of Limerick, but no one knows for certain where the name *limerick* comes from. Limericks are fun because they are short and silly, and have a bouncy, rhyming rhythm. They are easy to memorize and fun to recite. Writing your own limerick can be challenging because of the strict rhyming pattern, but students seem to enjoy the challenge and the silliness, regardless.

Features of a Limerick

- a short, silly, funny poem
- 5 lines
- no title
- distinct rhythm and rhyme
- rhyme pattern AABBA: lines 1, 2, and 5 rhyme; lines 3 and 4 rhyme
- first line usually includes a name or place
- last line is usually funny

ANCHOR BOOKS FOR LIMERICKS

Cleary, Brian P. *Something Sure Smells Around Here: Limericks*

Davis, Rod. *Out on a Limerick*
Longfellow, Chris. *Children's Limericks from A to Z*

ANCHOR POEMS FOR TEACHING LIMERICKS

"There was an Old Man from Nantucket" by Anonymous
"There Was an Old Man With a Beard" by Edward Lear

LESSON

- Share several limericks with students. Project or display, if possible, as it's helpful for them to see the format of the poem, as well as hear it, when you are reading it.
- Ask if anyone has heard of poems like this or knows the name of this kind of poem. Explain that this a well-known kind of poem called a *limerick*.
- Invite them to tell you what features they notice; what do the limericks have in common? (*5 lines; distinct rhyme and rhythm; often silly; usually about a person; person is usually introduced in the first line*)
- Tell students they will be writing limericks and that you are going to take them through the steps and give them some tips:

    Poets, today we are going to learn to write limericks. Limericks are poems that tell a short, silly story about a person. One of the most important features about a limerick is the rhythm and rhyming pattern.

- Explain that limericks have the rhyming pattern AABBA; i.e., Lines 1, 2, and 5 rhyme; lines 3 and 4 rhyme.
- Explain the district rhythm and practice clapping it:

    da DUM da da DUM da da DUM
    da DUM da da DUM da da DUM
    da DUM da da DUM
    da DUM da da DUM
    da DUM da da DUM da da DUM

- Continue the lesson:

   The first line of a limerick is the easiest to write because it almost always introduces a person and tells us their name or where they are from. The first line of a limerick usually ends with the person's name or a place. It helps if the person's name or the place is only one syllable, like Sue *or* Spain, *because that helps with the rhyming pattern.*

   Write the following two lines on the chart stand or board:

   There once was a lady named Sue (line ends with a name)
   There was an old woman from Spain (line ends with a place)

   Before writing any more of the poem, I need to consider rhyming words for either Spain *or* Sue. *I think I might have more luck finding words that rhyme with* Sue *so I'm going to make that my first line.*

- Invite students to help you brainstorm words that rhyme with *Sue* (*do, stew, shoe, flew, blew, blue, crew, moo, through*). List them on the board or chart stand. Remind them that lines 1, 2, and 5 all must rhyme.
- Look over the list of rhyming words and ask students if they can think of a funny story connected to them. They don't have to use all the words.

   I'm thinking that maybe this gal Sue likes making some weird kind of stew. The funny part is she ends up hitting something or someone with her shoe.

- Model writing all three rhyming lines first. This is not always necessary, but can help keep the storyline of the poem. Be sure to keep going back to the rhythm and model trying to find the words that match the beat. Leave a gap in the poem for lines three and four.

   There once was a lady named Sue
   Who liked to eat bumblebee stew
   (space for lines 3 & 4)
   And squashed them to bits with her shoe.

- Continue the lesson:

   Now I need to fill in lines three and four with something that makes sense. I also need to make sure that the lines rhyme and match the da-dum-da-da-dum *beat.*

- Invite students to help and talk through some of your own ideas and rhyming words:

   I think I need to include the word hive *here because, if she was making bumblebee stew, she would have to be near a hive. Now what rhymes with* hive?

- Complete the poem on the board:

   There once was a lady named Sue
   Who liked to eat bumblebee stew
   She waited outside

Just under a hive
Then squashed them to bits with her shoe.

- Invite students to read the limerick out loud with you. Clap out the rhythm to check that it matches the pattern.
- Tell students they will be writing their own limerick but, just before they do, you have one more limerick you would like them to read and discuss. Share this limerick:

There once was a tall man named Skip.
His favorite cookie was chocolate chip.
He had a big nose
And warts on his toes
And one day he did a big flip.

- Discuss the following with your students:

  - Does it have the correct structure? (*yes*)
  - Does it follow the rhyming rules of a limerick? (*yes*)
  - Does it have the correct rhythm? (*yes, for the most part*)
  - Does the poem tell a little story? (*no*)
  - Does the poem makes sense? (*no*)

Explain that, as with any kind of poem, the structure is important but, if the poem doesn't make sense, there is not much point!

- Pass out the Let's Write a Limerick! template on page 92. Remind students that the lines in their limerick need to all connect and tell a story, not just rhyme and have rhythm.

STUDENT SAMPLE POEM: LIMERICK

Grade 6

There once was a pig named Fred
Who spent every day in his bed.
The farmer got mad
And said he was bad
So he lay on the couch instead.

by Carla

Found Poetry

Found poetry can be described as the literary equivalent of a collage. A found poem is created when you "find" a poem in a piece of existing text. The poet "finds" existing words, phrases, or passages in a text and rearranges them to create an original poem.

Found poetry, like all poetry, can be written about anything and can be easily integrated into any content area. The pages of a class novel you are reading aloud, newspapers, magazines, a Craigslist ad, a famous poem, a page of Anne Frank's

Blackout poetry is a type of found poetry, but in reverse. Rather than extracting words from selected text to use to write a poem on a separate paper, the poet blacks out the words directly from the passage that aren't going to be part of the poem. The words that remain form the poem as well as a visual design.

I have not included any anchor books or anchor poems for this lesson as there really aren't any! Copyright of the primary source is often the issue and, without it, it's hard to appreciate how the poem emerged. There are examples on the internet if you search "Found Poetry for kids."

diary—primary text sources for creating found poetry are endless. One of the most fascinating things about practicing found poetry with your students is the number of unique poems that emerge from the same passage of text.

Features of a Found Poem

- uses words found from an existing text
- can include only words from the original text, but can repeat words
- can be about anything
- has meaning
- may or may not rhyme
- may include poetic devices, such as alliteration, imagery, and personification

---

ANCHOR BOOKS AS SOURCES FOR FOUND POETRY

The following are picture books I would recommend as primary resources because they include rich, detailed descriptions that work well for found poetry. Descriptive pages from novels also work well.

Brinckloe, Julie. *Fireflies*
Fletcher, Ralph. *Hello, Harvest Moon*
Fletcher, Ralph. *Twilight Comes Twice*
Hesse, Karen. *Come On, Rain*

Tresselt, Alvin. *White Snow, Bright Snow*
Van Allsburg, Chris. *The Polar Express*
Wells, Rosemary. *Night Sounds, Morning Colors*
Yolen, Jane. *Owl Moon* (page 79)

PREPARATION

Select your primary source for the found poetry and, if possible, project it. Alternatively, make enough hard copies so each student has one. You can use a page from a novel you are reading to the class, a page from a magazine or newspaper, a page from a nonfiction book, a famous poem (e.g., "Nothing Gold Can Stay" by Robert Frost or "The Raven" by Edgar Allan Poe). For the purpose of this lesson, I am using the classic book *Owl Moon* by Jane Yolen

LESSON

- Ask students if any of them like to collect things. Invite students to share what collections they might have: bugs, shells, rocks, marbles, hockey cards, nail polish. (I love rocks, so I would tell them about my rock collection.)
- Discuss the fact that some collections cost money and others are free: e.g., collecting hockey cards vs. collecting seashells.
- Ask students what they do with their collections (*keep them in a special box or book, display them, lock them in a drawer*).
- Show or project an example of a collage to the students. Explain that artists sometimes collect interesting objects and use them to create a piece of art called a collage.
- Tell students that poets can be collectors, too.

Poets are also collectors. Their treasures are words and they find them for free in unexpected places. Sometimes, they look for interesting words in nature; sometimes they might hear an interesting word on the bus; other times they find interesting words when they read. A poet might collect their favorite words in a notebook and use those words later to make a poem. This type of poem is called a found poem *because the poet is using words they found somewhere to write a poem.*

For copyright reasons, I am unable to include the actual page from *Owl Moon*, but the page begins with the text "We reached the line of pine trees, black and pointy…"

The first time I explain found poetry, I discuss the difference between *copying* words and *borrowing* words. Copying is when you use someone else's entire sentences or paragraphs exactly the way they wrote them and pretend that you wrote them. Borrowing is taking single words that someone wrote and rearranging them in your own unique way.

- Tell students that they will be learning how to write a found poem. Project or pass out copies of the primary source of text. For the purpose of this lesson, I have selected a passage from a page in *Owl Moon* by Jane Yolen.
- Explain that you are going to read through the passage and, while you are reading it, you are going to collect words you like in the passage and highlight them. Tell them you might like a word because of the way it's spelled, what it means, connections you make, or how it sounds.
- Begin to model the process, highlighting words and explaining your choices.
- Once you have finished collecting words from the page, explain that you are now going to make a list of the words you found on a separate paper.

pine	waited	face	sound
pointy	stars	silver	reading
sky	map	mask	reached
hand	moon	searching	

I recommend copying each word onto a separate index card so you can model how to play with different combinations as you rearrange the words into a poem.

- Read the list out loud and invite students to start thinking about how you could rearrange the words to make a poem. Explain that the poem you write may or may not be about owls. Discuss how you are looking for a theme or a message that you might want to write your poem about. For my list of words, I really liked the idea of "sky mapping" and wanted to try to make a poem about that.
- Begin writing your poem, inviting students to help you. Explain that you don't have to use all the words from the list.
- Explain that found poems should only include words from the original text, but repeating words is accepted. Depending on your grade, you may or may not want to follow this rule. I make exceptions when it comes to changing word endings. I refer to this as a "mini rule break!"
- The last step is to give your poem a title.

SAMPLE FOUND POEM BASED ON A PAGE FROM *OWL MOON* BY JANE YOLEN

Sky Maps by A. Gear

Silver moon waited.
Pointy stars searching,
Reading sky maps.

Pines mask sound
Face, hands searching.

Moon waits
Stars search
Sky maps.

- Pass out copies of additional primary sources or different pages from the same source (for this lesson, I might pass out different pages from *Owl Moon*).
- Pass out the Found Poetry Planner on page 93. Encourage students to double space when writing their word list so they can cut the words into strips, if they wish, which makes them easier to rearrange.

SAMPLE FOUND POEMS BASED ON FATTY LEGS BY CHRISTY JORDAN-FENTON AND MARGARET POKIAK FENTON

These samples were done by grade 5 students using different passages from the novel *Fatty Legs* by Christy Jordan-Fenton and Margaret Pokiak-Fenton. I selected different pages from significant moments in the story so that, when sequenced, the poems told the story. The poems were extremely powerful and moving.

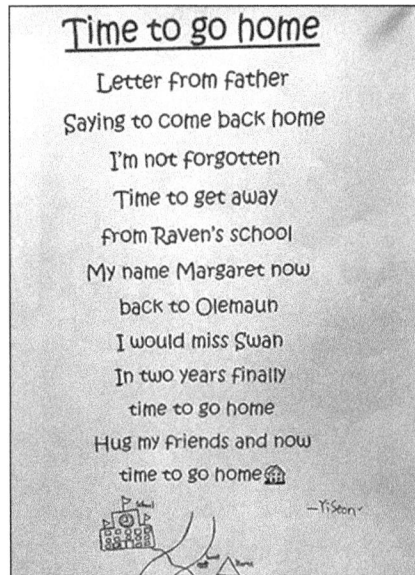

Time to go home

Letter from father
Saying to come back home
I'm not forgotten
Time to get away
from Raven's school
My name Margaret now
back to Olemaun
I would miss Swan
In two years finally
time to go home
Hug my friends and now
time to go home

—Tristan

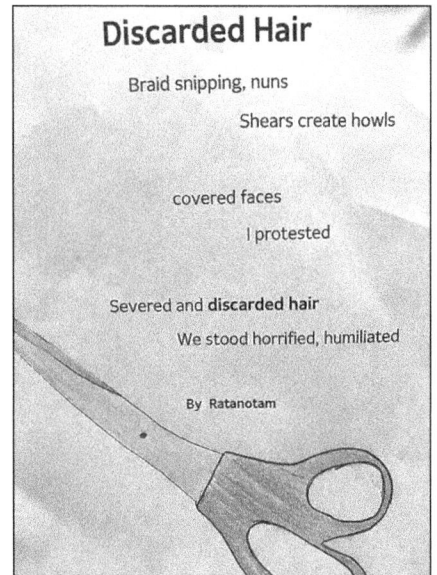

Discarded Hair

Braid snipping, nuns
Shears create howls

covered faces
I protested

Severed and **discarded hair**
We stood horrified, humiliated

By Ratanotam

Free Verse

Free verse is one of the simplest, yet most difficult, types of poetry to write and, therefore, to teach. Because there is no guiding frame or structure from which to build your poem, a poet must work exceptionally hard on creating a poem that is both meaningful and beautiful. I usually save free verse for later in the year, when students have developed a strong understanding of poetry and have learned several poetic devices they can apply to their free verse poems. I am often surprised and inspired when my students successfully write a poem free from rules, rhymes, and syllable count.

Features of Free Verse

- no poetic structure, frame, rhyming pattern, or syllable count
- no rules
- can include several poetic devices: repetition, personification, alliteration, onomatopoeia.
- can be about anything
- often leaves the reader with a feeling

Any book by Douglas Florian will include free verse poems

VanDerwater, Amy Ludwig. *Write! Write! Write!*

SUGGESTED ANCHOR POEMS FOR TEACHING FREE VERSE

"Dreamers" by Langston Hughes
"I Loved My Friend" by Langston Hughes
"Splishy, Sploshy Mud" by Ava Kent
"Thrill Ride" by Kenn Nesbitt
"Fog" by Carl Sandburg

LESSON

- Choose one or two free verse poems to share. For the purpose of this lesson, I use "I Loved My Friend" by Langston Hughes and "Thrill Ride" by Kenn Nesbitt. Both are available on the internet.
- Read the poem "I Loved My Friend" by Langston Hughes. Invite students to identify the 3 R's. (This will be challenging as there is no rhyming, no rhythm and only a little repetition.)
- Ask students what feeling they get when they read the poem (*sad, lonely*). Ask if the poet ever writes the word "sad" in the poem? (*no, but we get that feeling when we read it*)
- Read the poem "Thrill Ride" by Kenn Nesbitt. Ask students what they notice (*repetition, sound words, personification* in "hands grasp at the clouds")
- Ask students what they liked about it. (*words sound like the roller coaster clicking; we make connections, visualize*) What feeling did they get when they read it? (*excitement, scared, thrill*)
- Tell students that both of these poems are called free verse because the poet isn't following any particular structure, as they would if writing a haiku or list poem. In other words, they are "free" to write a poem completely on their own
- Explain that, because there is no structure, free verse can be a little harder to write, but that there are few things to consider before writing.

   First, you need to choose what your poem is going to be about. Remember you are free to choose anything— a feeling, a situation, an object, a person, or an event. I always recommend choosing a topic that interests you or you have a strong connection to.

- Model choosing a topic that interests you. (I have chosen campfires because it's my favorite part of camping—and I love camping!)
- Write your topic at the top of a chart stand or whiteboard.

   The next thing I want to do is think about the tone or feeling I want my poem to have. Tone is often connected to the topic you are writing about. For example, the roller coaster poem is fast-paced and exciting. The friend poem is sad and lonely. I think I want my poem to feel peaceful and magical, because that is how I feel when I'm sitting around a campfire at night.
   Now, I am going to start brainstorming words connected to my topic. I want to include descriptions, details, and especially some sensory word: sights, sounds, smells, etc.

- Model brainstorming words, inviting students to help you:

campfire	family	smell of burn-	night time
light	marshmallows	ing wood	stars
crackling	stars	clothes smell	laughter
smoke	warmth	camping	

- The next step is to do a *free write* using some of the ideas. Explain that you are not writing the poem yet, just writing a few sentences or phrases about your topic. Tell students you are trying not to write any feeling words, but want to describe the feelings.

> Crackling fire and the smell of smoke. We sit around and poke our sticks at the flames. We roast marshmallows and watch them get toasty brown and puffy. Who can cook the perfect marshmallow? We watch the sparks and the smoke rising up into the night. Finally, the flames go out and the orange embers are left. Bedtime. I love the smell of campfire on my clothes.

- Read the sentences out loud. Explain that, while you are reading, you are thinking about what words or phrases might be important for your poem or could be used as repeating words.
- Start with the first sentence but break it into smaller chunks to begin to write your poem on the chart stand or whiteboard. Write aloud, explaining when you might choose to include repetition, alliteration, or personification. Remind students that you don't have to follow a pattern or beat but you are trying to make it look, sound, and feel like a poem.

> **Campfire** by A. Gear
>
> Fire crackles
> Sparks speckle (*alliteration*)
> Smoke rises.
>
> The smell settles in my sleeves (*personification, alliteration*)
> Sticks poke at the flames
> The night air fills with memories and
> "remember when"s
>
> Laughter rises up with the smoke. (*personification*)
> Who will roast the perfect marshmallow?
> Toasty brown shell,
> Holding in the sweet goo.
>
> Sparks slow.
> Stars shine brighter
> As the embers fade. (*visual image*)
>
> Flashlights flicker. (*alliteration*)
> Zipping tents and sleeping bags. (*sensory: sounds*)
> The campfire follows me into the tent (*personification*)
> On my sleeves.

- Discuss the poetic devices you used. Emphasize the fact that your poem doesn't have a structure but still looks, sounds, and feels like a poem, and it tells a little story.

- Ask students if the poem gives them the feeling of being relaxed and happy by the fire, even though those words don't appear in the poem.

STUDENT SAMPLES

"Monkey Bars" Grade 4

"My Dog" Grade 2

Monkey Bars by Jana

Recess time
Some slide,
Some swing
But I climb!

Run! Run!
Don't stop until
you get there.

Reach up and grab the bars.
Cold like the doorknob to the
basement.

Climb to the very top and
Hang upside down.

All the kids down there
Standing on their heads!

Climbing down is not as fun.
Jump to the ground
From a few rungs up.
Legs like jelly.

Made it!

My Dog by Joshua

My dog
Wags her tail like a window wiper
When I get home from school.
Back and forth
Back and forth.

She licks my cheek
And tells me she missed me.
Back and forth
Back and forth.

I wonder what she does
All day
When I'm not here?

Let's Write Haiku!

Name: _____

> - a form of poetry originating in Japan
> - consists of 3 lines with a specific syllable count: 5-7-5
> - is usually about nature
> - usually includes a subject and an action

Step One: Choose a subject in nature for your poem.

I'm going to write about _____

Step Two: Write a sentence describing your topic in detail. Try to include an action.

_____

_____

_____

Step Three: Try to say it in a new way. Use personification or simile.

_____

_____

_____

Step Four: Now write your haiku. Use the 5–7–5 syllable count. Remember—you do not need a new idea on each line. Your sentence can flow into the line below.

_____

_____

_____

Pembroke Publishers © 2021 *Powerful Poetry* by Adrienne Gear ISBN 978-1-55138-352-1

Let's Write a Cinquain!

Name: _____

> • five lines long
> • has a 2-4-6-8-2 syllable count
> • is shaped like a diamond
> • often tells a little story
> • can include actions, feelings, and an ending
> • may or may not rhyme
> • can include poetic devices.

Step One: Choose a topic for your cinquain. (If possible, choose a word with two syllables.)

I'm going to write about _____

Step Two: Brainstorm ideas, words, and phrases connected to your topic

_____

_____

_____

Step Three: Look over your ideas. Try to find a story or a sequence. Write your poem, following the syllable sequence:

_____ (2)

_____ (4)

_____ (6)

_____ (8)

_____ (2)

Pembroke Publishers © 2021 *Powerful Poetry* by Adrienne Gear ISBN 978-1-55138-352-1

Diamante Poem

Name: _____

_____
Title

_____
topic

_____   _____
description   description

_____   _____   _____
action   action   action

_____ _____ _____ _____
four other nouns (person, place, or thing) that mean the same thing or are connected to the topic

_____   _____   _____
action   action   action

_____   _____
description   description

_____
another word that means the same as your topic

Acrostic Poem

Name: _____

What's the Scoop? Acrostic Poems

Name: _____

Single-Scoop Acrostic (one word for each letter)

_____

_____

_____

_____

_____

_____

Double-Scoop Acrostic (one sentence for each letter)

_____

_____

_____

_____

_____

_____

Triple-Scoop Acrostic (sentences can flow between lines, include personification, alliteration, simile)

_____

_____

_____

_____

_____

_____

Pembroke Publishers © 2021 *Powerful Poetry* by Adrienne Gear ISBN 978-1-55138-352-1

List Poem

Name: _____

_____

_____

_____

_____

_____

_____

_____

_____

_____

_____

_____

_____

_____

_____

_____

Concrete Poem Planning Page

Name: _____

Topic (try to think about a topic that has a simple shape): _____

Brainstorm words connected to your topic—think about action words, colors, sounds, smells, shapes, describing words.

_____	_____
_____	_____
_____	_____
_____	_____
_____	_____

Start with one or two sentences describing about your topic. Try to use personification or simile.

_____

_____

_____

Turn your ideas into a short poem.

_____

_____

_____

_____

_____

_____

Pembroke Publishers © 2021 *Powerful Poetry* by Adrienne Gear ISBN 978-1-55138-352-1

Concrete Poem Planning Page (cont'd)

Draw an outline of the shape of your topic in the box below. Copy your poem inside the shape, filling all the space.

Let's Write a Limerick!

Name: _____

Here are some things to remember about a Limerick:
- has five lines
- tells a little story
- 1st, 2nd, and 5th lines rhyme
- 3rd and 4th lines rhyme and are shorter
- rhythm is important and follows "ta-TUM-Ta" pattern
- 1st line usually introduces **a person** and **a place**
- last line usually repeats something from the first line

Step 1: Begin with the name of a place and a person. Find a rhyming word for each of the words.

Person: _____   rhymes with _____

Place: _____   rhymes with _____

Step 2: Choose the one with the easiest rhyming word. List other rhyming words here:

_____   _____   _____

_____   _____   _____

_____   _____   _____

Step 3: Look over your words and see if there is a little story you can find.

Step 4: Start writing! Try to write a limerick using the rules, rhythm and pattern. Remember, your limerick can be silly and fun!

First line for a person: There once was a _____ named _____

First line for a place: There once was a _____ from _____

Pembroke Publishers © 2021 *Powerful Poetry* by Adrienne Gear ISBN 978-1-55138-352-1

Found Poetry Planner

Name: _____

- List the words you found in your passage in the spaces below:

- Cut out your words. Look carefully at them. What do you notice? Are there any stories, themes, or messages you see?
- Start playing with different word combinations until you find something that might work for your poem. Arrange your words to look and sound like a poem.
- Write your poem on a new page. Remember you can repeat words and change endings to words, but try not to add new ones!

Pembroke Publishers © 2021 *Powerful Poetry* by Adrienne Gear ISBN 978-1-55138-352-1

4 Creating Poetry

"If there were to be a recipe for a poem, these would be the ingredients: word sounds, rhythm, description, feeling, memory, rhyme, and imagination. They can be put together a thousand different ways, and a thousand… thousand more." — Karla Kuskin

So, now what? You now have basically everything you need to bring poetry joy into your classroom, along with a wide range of lessons on poetic devices and techniques. You easily have enough lessons here for a successful poetry unit. But if I ended the book here, there would be nothing that sets it apart from other poetry resources. And if we are being honest, likely you could have found most of these lessons, in some form or another, on the Internet.

But I'm not finished! Far from it. In fact, I have left the best for last. Brain-pocket poetry! As I've said many times throughout this book, it's not enough to simply focus on poetry once a week for six weeks; teach your students how to follow the rules and write a haiku, acrostic, and cinquain; add some illustrations and staple them together into an anthology; and call it a day. Poetry should live everywhere in our classrooms and can be integrated into all aspects of our literacy programs, all year! Do not limit poetry to a six-week unit, because poetry is endless. It can easily connect to anything you are teaching because you can literally write a poem about anything! Brain-pocket poetry allows you to weave poetry into your writing program all year, based on what brain pocket you are focusing on.

What Are Brain Pockets?

Monday mornings are a popular time for journal writing. As a beginning teacher, not always completely organized for the new week, I would often use those first few minutes on Monday morning sorting myself out while my students wrote in their journals. (I hate to admit it, but that's what I did!) The journal entries would consist primarily of either bed-to-bed stories—"I woke up, I did this… I did that.. and then I went to bed"— or I Like… stories—"I like my mom. I like my dad. I like my dog. I like pizza. The end." The good thing about journal writing was that no teaching was required; the bad thing was that, eventually, you had to read them. And reading 26 journal entries was, let's be honest, painful!

I developed the idea of brain-pocket writing as an alternative to journal writing. Rather than have students write a list of what they did on the weekend, I introduce them to *brain pockets*—storage places in our brains that are filled with writing ideas. I explain that there are three major pockets in our brains that store our thinking: a memory pocket, a fact pocket, and an imagination pocket.

Writers use what they already have stored in their brain pockets as sources for their writing. Depending on what they are writing, they can search for ideas in one of their pockets. If they want to write about something that happened to them, for example, they would find that in their memory pocket; if they want to share information, they can use their fact pocket; if they want to write a made-up story, they can visit their imagination pocket.

Brain-pocket writing is much more interesting than journal writing and encourages students to explore different types of writing for different purposes. And best of all, students love it! It gives them freedom to choose what they write about, while providing them with some focus so that the blank paper staring up at them becomes far less daunting. Some students prefer to stay in one pocket (one student I know wrote about airplanes all year!), while others move between them.

What became clear to me after using brain-pocket writing was how closely tied brain pockets are to writing structures. In my most-recent book *Powerful Writing Structures*, I outlined the different writing structures that elementary students need experience with: personal narrative writing, nonfiction writing, story writing, and poetry writing. These different writing structures can be thought of in terms of brain pockets: we draw from our memory pocket when writing personal narrative; from our fact pocket when writing nonfiction; and from our imagination pocket when writing stories. Of course, there is always overlapping of pockets, as in historical fiction, or a book like *The Magic School Bus* that combines imagination and information. Generally, however, brain pockets help students understand different writing structures for different purposes.

The "secret sauce" of a good writing program is a combination of explicit instruction and application—in other words, lots of time to practice. I recommend spending several months focusing on each structure, allowing time for explicit instruction and a lot of opportunity for students to practice writing in that form. One of the questions I am asked frequently by teachers when it comes to organizing a writing program is, "How do I fit it all in?" How do you fit in the different writing structures, along with everything else you need to teach, in ten months? In my book *Powerful Writing Structures*, I suggest beginning the school year with personal narrative writing; mid-year is a focus on nonfiction writing; and story writing, the most complex of structures, I like to focus on at the end of the year when students have developed a little more competence and confidence in themselves as writers.

WRITING STRUCTURE YEAR PLAN

Term 1	Personal Narrative	Memory Pocket
Term 2	Nonfiction Writing	Fact Pocket
Term 3	Story Writing	Imagination Pocket
Term 1, 2 & 3	Poetry Writing	Memory, Fact, Imagination

Brain-Pocket Poetry Plan

Which brain pocket do writers draw from when writing poetry, you ask? The simple answer is… all three of them! You can write a poem from your memory pocket about your baby brother; a poem about an orca whale using your fact pocket; a poem about a unicorn based on your imagination pocket. So, while standard practice is teaching poetry as a separate writing unit, I like to sprinkle poetry throughout my year. After all, shouldn't the joy of poetry live in your classroom all year, and not just be limited to a few weeks' worth of lessons? Of course it should!

What I like about the "sprinkle" approach is how easily poetry can be integrated into all areas of your writing program and curriculum. While focusing on personal narrative writing, students can write poems based on their own memories and experiences: poems about family, friends, school, toys, food, pets... the possibilities are endless. When teaching nonfiction writing, students can write poems about animals, planets, the water cycle, or any content area you are covering. During your story writing unit, students can focus on their imagination pockets when they write poems.

Before teaching any writing lesson, it is important to clearly establish the following:

- **What is the topic?** (e.g., family fun, recess, feeling, water cycle, ladybugs)
- **What is the structure?** (e.g., personal narrative, nonfiction, story)
- **What is the target?** the specific writing technique that the students will practice (e.g., spacing, punctuation, interesting details, word choice)
- **What is the anchor book?** supporting either the topic or the target

The same questions can be asked when teaching a poetry lesson:

- **What is the topic?** (i.e. family fun, recess, feelings, water cycle, ladybugs)
- **What is the structure?** (e.g., haiku, list poem, acrostic poem, free verse, concrete poetry)
- **What is the target?** specific poetic device you might be integrating into the lesson teaching (e.g., simile, alliteration, rhyming, personification)
- **What is the anchor?** poem(s) to inspire the lesson or model a specific poetic device

Poetic structures and devices can be introduced within the context of the poetry lesson, but the topic of the poem can be linked to the writing structure and brain pocket you are already focusing on. This way, students will begin to see that the poems they write can focus on any topic and writing poetry can be done any time, not just in June.

TEACHING BRAIN POCKET POETRY

Writing Structure	Brain Pocket	Example Poetry Topics
Personal Narrative Writing	Memory Pocket	Family Feelings Friendship Community School
Nonfiction Writing	Fact Pocket	Animals Government Water cycle Interconnectedness of Nature

		Indigenous culture and beliefs
Story Writing	Imagination Pocket	Imaginary creatures Imaginary places Imagine you're a…

Memory-Pocket Poetry

Poets will tell you that the best poems come from ordinary experiences, objects, and memories, the "small moments" of life that can be transformed into something new. Memory-pocket poetry reinforces the fact that our memories are an infinite resource for writing. Writing poems from our own experiences allows us to bring to life the sounds, smells, and feelings of everyday things, opening up the possibility of turning the ordinary into something extraordinary. Memory-pocket poems also invite our readers make connections and create clear mental pictures.

The following poetry lessons invite students to use their memory pockets as the source for their poems. If you are already using memory pockets for personal narrative writing, weaving in memory-pocket poetry will be seamless. Most of these lessons refer back to previous lessons in the book for technique or structure; whenever that occurs, page references will be provided.

I Am From… Poem

Topic: Memories of home, family, culture
Structure: List poem (see page 69)
Target: Sensory details
Anchor Poem: "Where I'm From" by George Ella Lyon
Anchor Books:
Curry, Jennifer, ed. *Family Poems*
Greenfield, Eloise. *Brothers and Sisters: Family Poems*
Hoberman, Mary Ann. *Fathers, Mothers, Sisters, Brothers: A Collection of Family Poetry*

See pages 43–45 for the lesson on repetition.

This poetry lesson, a version of a bio poem, invites students to tap into their own personal memories to create a poem related to specific details and feelings about their family, home, culture, and traditions. It is a great lesson to introduce at the beginning of the school year to get to know your students.

- Write the word *house* on the board. Ask students what the word means (*building where people live*) Write the *home* on the board. Ask students what the difference is between the word *house* and the word *home*. (*house is the building; home is the people, events, feelings, memories connected to the building*)
- Invite students to spend a few moments in their memory pockets thinking about their home. What connections, feelings, and visual images come into their minds? Ten, twenty years from now, what will they remember most about their home?
- Share some of your own memories of your childhood home. Invite students to share their thoughts with a partner and/or with the class. Tell students that today they will be using some of those ideas and feelings to write a poem about their home and their family.
- Read aloud the poem "Where I'm From" by George Ella Lyon. Discuss specific poetic features such as repetition ("I am from…") and sensory details. Invite students to listen for the 3 R's and also to focus on some of the rich details they might use to visualize.
- Discuss how the poet is sharing very specific objects and memories from her memory pocket about where she is from, her childhood, her home, and her family.

- Point out that the poet did not add words *the* and *a* to the poem, making it sound more like a poem than a descriptive paragraph.
- Prepare the poem frame on a whiteboard or chart stand.

I am from _____(describe your home on the outside)

From _____(decorations or special objects inside)

I am from _____ (plants that grow near or in your house)

I am from _____(activities you do in the yard)

From _____ (activities your family does inside)

I am from _____(two favorite family foods or meals)

From _____(more special foods or drinks)

I am from _____(names of pets if you have them)

From _____ (names of 3 special toys or stuffies)

I am from _____(3 family celebrations)

I am from _____(2 special objects in your house)

From _____ (2 more objects)

I am from _____ (family country of origin, cultures)

From _____ (church or religion)

I am from _____(2 family traits)

Be sensitive to the fact that memories from home might not all be happy, and that sometimes writing can be a way of expressing feelings that may otherwise be hidden.

I recommend having planned your ideas before modeling!

- Explain that you are going to write your own I Am From… poem, using your ideas from your memory pocket. Invite students to be thinking about their own family and home while you model your own poem.
- Model a write-aloud, filling in the blanks while explaining your choices and sharing some memories. Like the anchor poem, avoid the words *the* or *a*, if possible.

I Am From by A. Gear

I am from grey steps, white paint with brown trim.
From orange shag, Edinburgh castle, and chandeliers
From warm peaches, purple plums, and runner beans.
I am from mud pies, badminton, and spying in the trees.
From monopoly, wheelbarrow, and basement roller skating.
I am from warm Shepherd's Pie and golden Yorkshire Puddings
From sweet shortbread, banana loaf, and Welsh cakes.

I am from Jock, Tigger, Dougal, and Janie.
From Ketchup, Pink Snoopy, and Raggedy Anne.
I am from Christmas, Robbie Burns Day, and Easter egg hunts
I am from tartan Kilts, clicking knitting needles, and highland dancing swords
From Christmas ornaments and Brigadoon dishes.
I am from England, Scotland, and Canada
From the Sunday school, carol practice, and church lady lunches.
I am from singing, snoring, and storytelling
I am from laughter and love.

I have modified this I Am From… lesson to make it easier for younger writers. You can find a more advanced version for older writers at http://www.georgeellalyon.com/where.html and there are many online including: https://freeology.com/worksheet-creator/poetry/i-am-from-poem/

- Pass out the I Am From… template on page 134. Encourage students to think about how they would express what their home looks or their favorite toy means to them with simple but vivid images, conveying how they look, smell, feel, etc.

Topic: Family members, community
Structure: List poem (see page 69)
Target: Vocabulary, triple-scoop words
Anchor Poem: "I'm Talking Big!" by Colin McNaughton

I'm Talking… Poem

Colin McNaughton's poem "I'm Talking Big!" is jam-packed with triple-scoop words, so it is a perfect one to build vocabulary and encourage students to be more adventurous with their word choice. It's also a poem that lends itself well to many different memory-pocket extensions.

- Share the poem with students. If possible, copy it out onto chart paper or project it onto the screen so that the students can become familiar with the formatting.
- Ask students what they notice about the poem. (*repetition; lots of triple-scoop words; number of triple-scoop words gets longer each line—3,4,5, etc.; feeling of excitement building as the list of words gets longer*)
- Explain that the poet chose a single-scoop word (*big*) and then included many different words that mean the same or almost the same thing. Depending on your grade, you might want to introduce the concept of synonyms—words that share the same meaning—and a thesaurus, or dictionary of triple-scoop words!
- Tell students that they are going to practice writing a mini synonym poem. Invite them to think of some single-scoop words; e.g., *walking, hot, small, happy, good, cold, sad, mad.*
- Copy the I'm Talking… poem frame on the board.

I'm Talking _____

I'm talking _____ (repeat the title)

I'm talking _____ (1 synonym)

I'm talking _____, _____ (2 synonyms)

I'm talking _____, _____, _____ (3 synonyms)

I'm talking _____ (repeat the title)

Introducing students to a thesaurus would be a great addition to this lesson.

Invite students to help you complete the poem:

I'm talking HOT
I'm talking burning!
I'm talking steaming, sweating!
I'm talking roasting, sizzling, blistering.
I'm talking hot!

• Invite students to choose a single-scoop word and, with a partner or on their own, create a synonym poem.

I'm Talking Small by Travis

I'm talking small
I'm talking tiny!
I'm talking miniscule, baby-sized.
I'm talking miniature, compact, need a microscope.
I'm talking small!

• Once the students have had practice with the poem frame, it can easily be adapted to many different memory-pocket topics. I enjoy using it with primary students when we are focusing on special grown ups in our lives: mums, dads, grandparents. Use the I'm Talking Family Member (Primary) template on page 135 and write-aloud, modeling your ideas before having the students complete theirs.

I'm Talking Dad

I'm talking Dad!
I'm talking Popo
I'm talking smart, funny, athletic.
I'm talking taxi driver, hockey coach, lawn cutter, dog walker
I'm talking laughing, snoring, singing, tickling, fixing
I'm talking amazing, tremendous, legendary, epic, fantastic, extraordinary
I'm talking love!
I'm talking Dad!

I'm Talking Mom

I'm talking Mom
I'm talking Mummy
I'm talking kind, smart, loving
I'm talking teacher, reader, clothes washer, cook
I'm talking reading, hiking, dog walking, hugging, laughing
I'm talking amazing, stupendous, legendary, special, excellent, unforgettable
I'm talking love.
I'm talking Mom

EXTENSION

This frame also works well linked to Our Community" After brainstorming landmarks and important places the students know and spend time in the local community, students can create a I'm Talking… connected to their neighborhood.

I'm Talking Main Street

I'm talking Main Street
I'm talking Queen Elizabeth Park
I'm talking Sexsmith School, Sunset Community Center, Riley Park
I'm talking farmers market, Nat Bailey Stadium, Nesters Market, Hillcrest Pool, Helen's Grill
I'm talking block parties, garage sales, baseball games, picnics in the park.
I'm talking neighborhood.
I'm talking HOME!

Family Metaphor Poem

Topic: Family
Structure: Free verse (see page 80)
Target: Metaphor (see page 39)
Anchor Poem: "Earth Head" by Ralph Fletcher

See page 39 for the lesson on metaphor.

Ralph Fletcher's poem "Earth Head" is a perfect anchor for introducing the concept of metaphor to young poets. Describing a baby's head as the earth is not only clever, but is also simple enough for your students to visualize and connect to it. If you have not yet taught the technique lesson on Metaphor (page 39), I would recommend teaching that lesson prior to this one.

- Read aloud Ralph Fletcher's poem "Earth Head." Discuss how he uses the metaphor of a globe to describe his baby brother's head. Remind students that a metaphor is a poetic technique by which the poet compares a topic to something that is different, but that shares some of the same characteristics; e.g., a baby's head is the earth, the baby's hair is the arctic tundra.
- Explain that students are going to be writing a poem about their family, using a metaphor. The topic they choose will represent their family and the subtopics will represent each family member.
- Brainstorm topics to use for their metaphors. Encourage them to think of a topic that has several subtopics:

  Groceries: apples, meat, cheese, fruit, bread
  Car: motor, steering wheel, radio, wipers, gas
  Medicine cabinet: band-aid, tweezers, pain pill, thermometer
  Kitchen utensils: fork, spoon, knife, flipper, whisk
  Tools: hammer, wrench, screwdriver, saw, nails
  Buildings: house, tent, skyscraper, apartment, doghouse
  Books: adventure, romance, mystery, horror, fantasy
  Shoes: high heels, runners, flip-flops, hiking boots, steel-toed boots

- Choose a topic and model how to match family members to different items, based on their personality.

  "My family is a bookshelf"
  Dad = mystery
  Mom = detective novel
  Sister = dystopian fiction
  Brother = adventure
  Grandma = fantasy
  Me = thriller

- Model a write-aloud, adding details to explain the family metaphors. Remind students that a metaphor is a statement, so they don't need to explain their connections.; e.g., "My dad is a mystery. You never know what he's thinking" rather than "My father is a mystery because you never know what he's thinking." Also remind them that they do not need to use the words *as* or *like* because they are not writing similes.

- Pass out the Family Metaphor Planning Page on page 136 and invite students to use it to create their own poem.

Metaphor for a Family

My family is a bookshelf.
Dad is a mystery.
You never quite know what he's thinking
Mom is the detective, quietly looking for clues
And solving everything for us.
My sister is dystopia – a little weird and hard to explain.
My little brother is the adventure, looking for fun in every corner.
My grandma is the fantasy. She can't really remember things so
she makes them up.
I am the thriller full of surprises, excitement, and keeping everyone
On the edge of their seat!

This kind of metaphor poem can be also written about different types of friends. Douglas Florian's poetry book *Friends and Foes: Poems About Us All* is an excellent anchor for writing memory-pocket poems about friends.

STUDENT SAMPLE POEMS: FAMILY METAPHOR

My family is like a Christmas tree:

My dad is the Christmas tree always holding our love.
My little sister Evan is the candy cane with big sweet tooth always eating her candy.
Mom is the ornaments so pretty and bright.
My older sister Kailee is the star at the top shinning brightly.
I am the stem growing the love in our family.

Metaphor for a Family by Belinda, Grade 6

My family lives inside a medicine chest:
Dad is the super-size band aid, strong and powerful
but not always effective in a crisis.
Mom is the middle-size tweezer,
which picks and pokes and pinches.
David is the single small aspirin on the third shelf,
sometimes ignored.
Muffin, the sheep dog, is a round cotton ball, stained and dirty,
that pops off the shelf and bounces in my way as I open the door.
And I am the wood and glue which holds us all together with my love.

When I Was Young Poem

Topic: Memories, community/city/town

Structure: Free verse (see page 80)

Target: Repetition (page 43), sensory details (page 31), simile (page 37), alliteration (page 45)—any poetic technique

Anchor Books:

Curtis, Jamie Lee. *When I Was Little*

MacLachlan, Patricia. *All the Places to Love*

Rylant, Cynthia. *When I Was Young in the Mountains*

One of my very earliest educational mentors was David Booth, a beloved Canadian educator, professor, speaker, and author. Years after hearing him present for the first time, I was fortunate enough to call him my friend. Very early in my career, I attending a conference where he was speaking to teachers about inspiring our young writers. He shared a writing lesson using Cynthia Rylant's book *When I Was Young in the Mountains*. This was a pivotal moment in my teaching career, as I witnessed first-hand the power of a picture book to inspire a lesson. I am forever grateful to David Booth for sharing this lesson, and honored to be passing on his love of poetry and picture books to other teachers and their students.

- Choose an anchor book, preferably *When I Was Young in the Mountains* by Cynthia Rylant.
- Before reading it aloud, tell students that this story is about someone thinking about when they were younger and sharing memories from their memory pocket of people and places. Invite students to listen for the repetition and sensory detail in the story.
- Read the anchor book aloud.
- After reading, discuss the repeating line, "When I was young in the mountains." Explain to students that they will be writing a poem about memories they have of their home and special places they remember.
- Model by telling students where you grew up. Explain that, when you think of this place, you have lots of memories of growing up there in your memory pocket. Share some memories with your students, listing a few activities you did with your family when you were younger. Try to connect an activity with a specific location.

> *I grew up in Vancouver. When I was young in Vancouver I remember…*
>
> - *eating fish and chips at Spanish Banks with my family*
> - *playing in Queen Elizabeth Park*
> - *watching the donut machine in Oakridge Mall*
> - *the train in Stanley Park*
> - *riding my bike around the track at the park*
> - *collecting chestnuts on Blenheim Street*
> - *playing in the back yard with my sisters*

- Invite students to think about activities and places they remember going to with their friends and family (park, community centre, restaurant, beach, grandparent's house). Ask them to share a few of these memories with a partner. Invite a few to share out with the class.
- Explain they will be writing a memory-pocket free-verse poem (see lesson on page 80) about these places, using the same repeating line from the story.
- Model using some of the ideas from your list to write a free verse poem:

> When I was young in Vancouver
> I remember
> Summer suppers on the beach.
> Fish and chips and vinegar,
> Seagulls sometimes snatched
> My chips.

When I was young in Vancouver
I remember
Queen Elizabeth Park picnics
Tiny twigs race down the river
Sisters following and running beside.
Whose stick will win?

- Discuss the pattern, the stanzas, and the alliteration you tried to include. Point out that you were trying not to write a story, so you didn't write long sentences. You tried to make your lines short, like a poem.
- Pass out the When I was Young template. Invite students to start by listing special memories of when they were younger at the top of the page. At the bottom, invite them to use create their free verse poem using short lines, repetition, and alliteration.

STUDENT SAMPLE POEM: WHEN I WAS YOUNG

Grade 5

When I Was Young In Kelowna

When I was young in Kelowna
I remember
Sitting on the Ogopogo
Holding on tight to the scales
Scared it was real.

When I was young in Kelowna
I remember
Summer at the beach
Running on the hot sand
Ahhhh... feet in the water feels good.

When I was young in Kelowna
I remember
Picking cherries from
Granpa's tree
Wearing cherry earings.

ALTERNATIVE

Older students could choose to focus on a single memory and really develop it using sensory details:

When I was young in Vancouver,
Summers at Spanish Banks Beach.
Sisters dig rowboats in the sand
Wood planks for seats
And away we row.

Fish and chips and malt vinegar.
Seagulls screech and snatch.
Fudgesicles follow on the log.
Sun setting, sand sticking.
Brush off the sand, girls.
Sleepy Streetlights from the car window.
When I was young in Vancouver.

Poems About Feelings

"Poetry is when an emotion has found its thought and the thought has found words." – Robert Frost

Topic: Feelings
Structure: Free verse (see page 80)
Target: "Show, don't tell"
Anchor Poem: "My Friend" by Langston Hughes

Our memory pockets are filled with memories, each memory attached to a feeling. Feelings become a universal thread through many poems. Good poets evoke feelings without ever having written a "feeling" word. Often, it is what a writer doesn't say that leaves us with the strongest feelings. While we may be all familiar with the expression "show, don't tell," we might not be aware how much value it holds when teaching students how to write a powerful poem.

- Read aloud the poem "My Friend" by Langston Hughes. Ask students what the poem means. Ask students what they are wondering about the poem. (*did the friend move? pass away? start hanging out with someone else?*)
- Discuss the 3 R's. (*only a little repetition in* "I loved my friend.")
- Ask students what feeling they get when they read the poem. (*sad, lonely*)
- Tell students that sometimes poets write about something that is emotional, but they don't actually name the feeling in their poem. They write something that a reader might make a connection to and might cause them to find the feeling in their memory pocket.

> *I might read this poem and think about the time when my best friend Nicola moved to a new school in Grade 3. She used to live right down the street and then she was gone. I remember being really sad about that. So this poem makes me think about that.*

- Explain that not all poems are happy and cheerful. Sometimes poems can be about sad or disappointing things because everyone has experiences like that. Writing can sometimes help you not feel so sad anymore.
- Begin to brainstorm a list of feeling words. You might want to focus on positive and negative feelings.

SAMPLE FEELINGS BRAINSTORM

Positive Feelings	Negative Feelings
Excited	Sad
Happy	Lonely
Proud	Disappointed
Grateful	Embarrassed
Surprised (in a good way!)	Scared
Calm	Mad
Relaxed	Worried

- Invite students to go into their memory pockets and find a time when they experienced one of the feelings. Model your own:

I felt sad when my dog Bailey died. She got really sick really quickly, and the vet said that they couldn't save her, and then she died. She was my best friend. I cried for a week. I kept turning a corner in the house and thinking she would be there. But she wasn't.

- Invite students to think for a few minutes and then to share their feeling memory with a partner. Invite some to share with the class.
- Tell students they will be writing a poem about a feeling, but the most important thing is that they are not allowed to name the feeling by writing the feeling word in the poem.
- Explain that the poem is going to be written as a free verse, but that they should try to include such things as repetition, simile, and alliteration. The most important thing is to try to help the reader "feel the feeling" without actually writing the feeling word in the poem.
- Pass out the Feeling Poem template on page 138. Explain that, after choosing their feeling, students are to write a few sentences, just to get the ideas out of their memory pockets. Once they have an idea of what they want to say, they can begin to write the feeling poem, being careful not to write the feeling word.

Bailey by A. Gear

Bailey got sick.
She was fine,
Then she wasn't.
The vet said there was nothing she could do,
Nothing she could do.

Bailey got sick
And then she died.
And then she was gone.
My shoulders went up and down, up and down
Like a pogo stick
When I cried.
I cried a lot.

I looked for her in the kitchen,
But she wasn't there.
I guess she's gone from my kitchen,
But not from my heart.

"My Pillow" by Maria, Grade 2
"Covid" by Henrietta, Grade 3

Lonely Pillow

When I was four
I had a pillow.
It was blue and it had
a face.
    One day I bought a stuffy
I loved it!
I thought that I loved the
stuffy more.
My pillow just sat there
feeling alone.
So I played with them both.

by Maria

Covid   by Henrietta
Covid came one day
We didn't invite it.
It just arrived.
Then we had to
stay home
stay home
stay home

No playing
No fun
No friends
No visiting Oma
You mite make her sick.

I miss her warm hands
that smell like roses
I hope I can smell
roses again soon.

Gratitude Poem

Topic: Gratitude
Structure: Haiku (see page 59)
Target: Personification (see page 41), simile (see page 37)
Anchor Book:
Paul, Miranda, ed. *Thanku: Poems of Gratitude*

Often, we save thank-you poems for Thanksgiving, inviting our students to write a list of things they are grateful for. But expressing gratitude should not be limited to one day a year. Reminding our students of their good fortune and encouraging them to show and share gratitude can be a year-round practice. While Thanksgiving poems are often a list of things we are grateful for, this lesson uses the structure of a haiku poem.

- Write the word *gratitude* on the board. Ask students what it means. Ask them for other words that mean the same thing (*thankfulness, appreciation*).
- Ask students what they are grateful for (*people, pets, toys, nature, friends, food*). List their responses on the board.
- Share some of the poems from *Thanku: Poems of Gratitude*. If you don't have a copy of the book, there are several videos of poems from this book being read aloud on YouTube.

If you have not taught haiku, I recommend teaching the lesson on page 60 first.

- Explain to students that they will be writing a poem of gratitude. Tell them they will be using the haiku poem structure.
- Review the features of haiku (*3 lines; 5-7-5 syllable count;, often includes personification and simile*). Remind students that, because haiku poems do not have many words, the challenge for poets is to choose their words carefully.
- Guide students to choose something from their memory pocket that they are grateful for. Encourage them to think of something that is very special to them—a person, pet, object, place. Remind them that haiku is often about nature, so to avoid topics like video games or pizza.
- Model how to start by writing a few ideas in sentences or phrases about your topic, without focusing on syllable count:

    I am grateful for hiking in the woods. I like the smell of the forest and the feel of the pinecones and pine needles under my feet. I like the way the air feels and breathing in the smell.

See page 41 for the lesson on Personification; page 37 for the lesson on Simile.

- Explain that the next step is focusing on the syllables and trying to include simile or personification. Remind students that one sentence can take up two lines. Tell them that the two important words to include in their poem are their topic and a gratitude word: *grateful, thankful, thank-you, appreciate, appreciative.* (Note that the word *appreciative* has five syllables, so would be the only word on line 1 or 3.)

> Hiking in the woods,
> I breath in the cool forest.
> Pine cone steps. Grateful.

- Pass out the Gratiku: Gratitude Haiku template on page 139. Invite students to create their own gratitude poems.

STUDENT SAMPLE POEMS: GRATITUDE HAIKU

"dog" By Karin, Grade 2
"Auntie Cheryl" By Jes, Grade 4

thankful for my dog
her tail is a wiper,
back and forth it goes.
by Josh

My auntie Cheryl
Sends me funny texts
rapped in love. Gratful.
by Jes

Apology Poem

Topic: Apology
Structure: Free verse (see page 80)
Target: Direct address
Anchor Poem: "This is Just to Say"
by William Carlos Williams
Anchor Books:
Levine, Gail Carson. *Forgive Me, I Meant to Do It: False Apology Poems*
Sidman, Joyce. *This is Just to Say: Poems of Apology and Forgiveness*

Joyce Sidman's brilliant book *This is Just To Say* is a collection of both sincere and sarcastic, tongue-in-cheek apology poems that inspired this lesson. Most of these poems are in the form of *direct address*, meaning that the speaker in the poem (the poet) is speaking directly to a specific person or object. Apology poems are a great way for students to find their voice and use it in a sincere or not-so-sincere apology.

- Write the word *apology* on the board or whiteboard. Ask students what the word means. Ask them why they think it's sometimes hard for people to apologize. (*hard to admit you are wrong, feel badly*)
- Invite them to search their memory pocket and think of a time when they either made an apology or knew they should have but didn't. Have them discuss with a partner or the class.
- Remind students that there are many different kinds of poems—poems that are funny, poems that give us feelings, poems that describe interesting images. Explain that some poems can actually talk to you. These poems are ones that use *direct address*, meaning the poet is talking directly to someone else so that you can hear their voice.
- Tell students that an apology poem is a one that uses direct address as a way for the speaker in the poem to apologize for something that they have said or done.
- Share the poem "This is Just to Say" by William Carlos Williams. (This poem is easily accessible on the Internet). Explain that this is one of the most famous examples of an apology poem. Written in 1938, it was the first time someone had ever written a poem about saying sorry. Invite readers to think about who the speaker might be apologizing to and what they are apologizing for.

- Ask students what action has happened (*someone ate plums that someone else was saving*). Ask them if they think the speaker is truly sorry for what they did? (*No, because they spent a lot of time describing how good the plums tasted.*)
- Discuss the fact that the speaker doesn't seem too sincere about their apology because of the way they described how delicious the plums were. Introduce the terms *sincere apology* (you are truly sorry) and *insincere apology* (you are saying sorry but you don't really mean it).
- Invite students to search their memory pocket and remember a time when they were told to apologize but they didn't really mean it (insincere), and a time when they apologized for something that they truly felt sorry they had done (sincere). Invite students to share with a partner or with the class.
- Tell students they are going to write an apology poem and write it as if they are apologizing directly to someone. Students can choose either a sincere or insincere apology poem.
- Use the Apology Poem template on page 140 to model:

> *First, I think I'm going to choose an insincere apology poem. I remember a time when I knocked over my sister's sandcastle. My mum made me apologize but I wasn't really sorry because my sister hadn't let me help her so I was mad at her.*

(write a short description of the action)

> *Now I am going to think of the sensory detail—the sight, taste, smell, sound, or touch that will give my readers the impression that I am not really sorry.*

(model)

> *Now I think I'm ready to write my apology poem. I'm going to borrow the pattern from the plum poem and use very short lines and no punctuation. I'm going to start with "This is just to say" and end with "Forgive me. I'm going to try to group my lines into stanzas and maybe try to include some alliteration.*

I'm Sorry by A. Gear

This is just to say
that I have stepped
on your sandcastle
you spent all afternoon
building
without me

I watched you fill each bucket
with damp sand
and patiently pat
the tall towers
without me

The sand tickled my toes
When the castle collapsed.
Forgive me.

- Discuss your repetition of "without me" and the alliteration "patiently pat," "tall towers," "tickled my toes."

- Remind students that there is no wrong way to write an apology poem. They can borrow the format from William Carlos Williams or create something on their own.

STUDENT SAMPLE POEMS: APOLOGY POEMS

"I'm Sorry" (insincere apology), Grade 6

"My Fist" (sincere apology), Grade 4

I'm Sorry

This is just to say
I'm sorry
For drinking your slurpee
When you went to the bathroom

I was so hot and you
Got to go to 7-11 with dad
While I was at soccer practice

I was so hot
And cream soda and orange crush
Is my favorite.

The icy sweetness
Tickled my tongue
And really cooled me down.
Forgive me.

My Fist

I'm sorry for hitting you.
I wanted to hit you
Because I was mad
But after I hit you
I felt bad.

You cried and
Then your face went all red
And then the tears
Squeezed out of eyes like a lemon.
And you held your arm
Where my fist landed

I wanted to say sorry
But my words got lost
Somewhere
So I just stood there.
But now I found my words inside
this pencil
I'm sorry.

EXTENSION

For added creativity, students can apologize to an inanimate object rather than directly to a person. They can think of everyday objects they use and what they would say to the if the object could understand.

STUDENT SAMPLE POEM: APOLOGY TO AN OBJECT

Grade 2

I'm Sorry

I'm sorry, Pencil
I didn't mean to keep grinding you
smaller and smaller.

But Mrs. gear
Likes me to have a sharp pencil.
For printing my poems.
I'm relly sorry, Pencil.
Does it hurt alot?
Do you get lonely at night in the Desk
by yourself?

Noisy Place Poem

Topic: Noisy places
Structure: Free verse (see page 80)/ List poem (see page 69)
Target: Onomatopoeia (see page 47)
Anchor Poem: "Weather is Full of the Nicest Stounds" by Mary Ann Hoberman
Anchor Books:
Heidbreder, Robert. *Noisy Poems for a Busy Day*
Bennett, Jill, ed. *Noisy Poems*

Memory-pocket poems that focus on sounds can help students practice the technique of onomatopoeia while writing about a place they are familiar with. These poems appeal to the sense of hearing, bringing the poem to life in the reader's mind.

- Tell students that they are going to be writing Noisy Place Poems. Invite them to go into their memory pockets and think of places that are noisy. Brainstorm ideas with the class and create a list on the board:

Noisy Places

hockey rink	kitchen
street	lunchroom
library (even though it's supposed to be quiet there are still sounds!)	park
	amusement park
restaurant	school ground at recess
grocery store	classroom

- Explain that after they choose their noisy place, they will need to list the specific objects or things that make noise in that place. Model, using one of the ideas from the list:

Kitchen Sounds

Pots and pans	Eggs
Bacon	Toaster
Knifes and forks	Spoon
Mom	Water

See page 47 for the lesson on Onomatopoeia.

- Tell students that they are going to be using onomatopoeia in this poem. Remind them that this technique is when a poet replaces an action word with a sound word. For example, instead of saying "the bacon is cooking," the poet would write "Sizzle! Sizzle! Pop!"; instead of saying "the kettle is boiling," you could write "Phsssssssss!"
- Remind students that, since the sound word replaces the action word, they should try not to include action words. Go back to the list and add the sound word beside each object. Invite students to help you. Tell them not to worry about spelling for some of the sound words.

Pots and pans – Clink! Clank! Bang!
Bacon – Sizzle Sizzle, pop pop!
Knifes and forks – tink tink clink
Eggs – Kik! Fffllop
Toast – pop!
Spoon – tinkley tink, tinkley tink
Water – drip… drip
Kettle – Whiiiiiiieeee!
Mom – "Breakfast is ready!"

- Once you have your list of sound words, explain that the poem needs to tell a little story. Tell the students that sounds in a kitchen might be someone cooking breakfast so you are going to call your poem "Noisy Breakfast."

Noisy Breakfast

Growl! Growl! I'm hungry!
Clank! Bang crash … Where is the frying pan?
Bacon in. Sizzle! Sizzle! Pop!
Ouch! That's hot!
Crrrrrrack! ZZZZzzzzz! Egg is in.
Whhiiiiieeeee! Coffee's almost ready.
Pop! Up comes the toast!
"Breakfast!"
Click clack plate scrape.
Yummmmmm! My tum is full!
Time to start my day.

- Pass out the Noisy Place Poem Planner on page 141. Remind students to first list the noisy objects and the sound words connected to each. Once they have their list, they can use the ideas to write a poem that tells a little story.

STUDENT SAMPLE POEMS: NOISY PLACES

Both these poems were written by a Grade 4 student who took a great liking to writing sound poetry!

Noisy Lunchroom

CRASH! The food trays clatter
CLAP! CLAP!
RiP! Lunch bags open.
Munch! Crunch!
Yum! Yum!
Slurp! Sip!
Juice whoosh!
Finish your food!
Shhhh too loud!
Plunk don't forget to recycle!
Toss - two points!
Time to play outside!
Yah!

Noisy Pizza
by Calvin

Swirl! Twirl!
Dough in the air.
Splat! Splosh!
Sauce on the dogh.
Sprinkle, spread
Cheese on top.
Flip! Toss!
Pepperoni on the cheese
Slide Slip
Pizza in the oven
Sizzle sizzle!
Bubbily cheese
Yum! Yum!
Delicious noisy pizza!

Topic: Color
Structure: List poem (see page 69)
Target: Senses, simile (see page 37), repetition (see page 43)
Anchor Books:
Jonas, Ann. *Color Dance*
O'Neill, Mary. *Hailstones and Halibut Bones*
Seeger, Laura Vaccaro. *Green* (also *Blue* and *Red*)
Seuss, Dr. *My Many Colored Days*
Sidman, Joyce. *Red Sings From Treetops*
Yolen, Jane. *Color Me a Rhyme*

Six Senses of Color Poem

It's hard to write a poetry book without including a lesson on color poems! And it's equally hard to teach a lesson on color poems without a copy of *Hailstones and Halibut Bones* by Mary O'Neill! If you don't have a copy, your school library is almost sure to have one. This modern classic is almost 60 years old and features rich, luminous poems about the beautiful colors that surround us. This lesson invites students to explore colors and the smells, tastes, sounds, and feelings associated with them. These color poems also lend themselves well to incorporating metaphor. Using paint chips is a fun, creative way of having your students present their poem.

- Write the word *green* on the board. Invite students to go into their memory pocket and think of as many things as they can think of that are green. Have them share and compare their ideas with a partner.
- Come together as a class and create a class list. Record words on the board or chart stand. Draw students' attention to the fact that the majority are things that we see are green. But what about how green smells? Tastes? Feels? What about the senses of green?
- Read *Green* by Laura Vaccaro Seeger or "Green" from Mary O'Neill's *Hailstones and Halibut Bones* to students. (Check YouTube for these read-alouds)
- Invite students to listen for the senses associated with the color while you read the poem. Explain that we see color, but we also taste and smell and feel color.
- Create a Senses of Color chart on the board and invite students to help you complete it. Remind students that scientists acknowledge five senses, but poets and writers have six because they include emotions. Explain that different colors often remind us of different feelings; e.g., red – mad, excited; yellow – happy, cheerful, hot.

SAMPLE: SIX SENSES OF GREEN

Sight	Grass, trees, parrots, frogs, broccoli, turtles, cucumbers
Smell	Lime, grass, pine needles
Sound	Wind through trees
Taste	Sour lime, sour Granny Smith apple, bitter matcha
Touch	Soft grass, prickly pine needles, smooth apple, bumpy broccoli
Feelings	calm, hopeful, quiet, cool

- Pass out the Six Senses of Color planner on page 142. Invite students to choose a color and begin to add ideas to the planner. Encourage them to choose less popular colors like black, white, and brown. We don't want those colors to feel left out!
- Once students have completed their plan, explain that they are going to use some of their ideas to create a color poem. Tell them that they will be writing a list poem and using the poetic technique of metaphor. Remind students that a metaphor is when a poet makes a comparison between two things that aren't alike but share something in common.
- Explain to students that, for this poem, they will be comparing the color to their senses and adding details. Model:

See page 39 for the lesson on Metaphor.

Other poetic device options for this poem would be simile—*Green is like the sour smell of lime* —or personification—*I am the smell of the fresh green grass.*

The Six Senses of Green

Green is a tall tree stretching its branches to the sky
Green is the smell of fresh grass, damp and sticking to my shoes.
Green is a soft wind blowing.
Green is a sour lime making my lips squeeze and pucker
Green is prickly pine needles on my Christmas tree

Green is a peaceful forest.
Green

- Discuss how you used a metaphor and started each line with *Green is*…. Explain how you added details to each line. Instead of just writing *Green is a tall tree*, you added a detail. Also discuss that there were no repeating ideas— each line was a new idea.
- When students are finished their poems, one option is to have them create Paint Chip Poems by writing their poems onto paint chip cards. I recommend Behr samples because they are large and provide enough space for students to write. The finished poems look very colorful on display! I recommend having a few silver gel pens on hand for when the color chips are too dark to write on.

STUDENT SAMPLE POEM: PAINT CHIP POEM

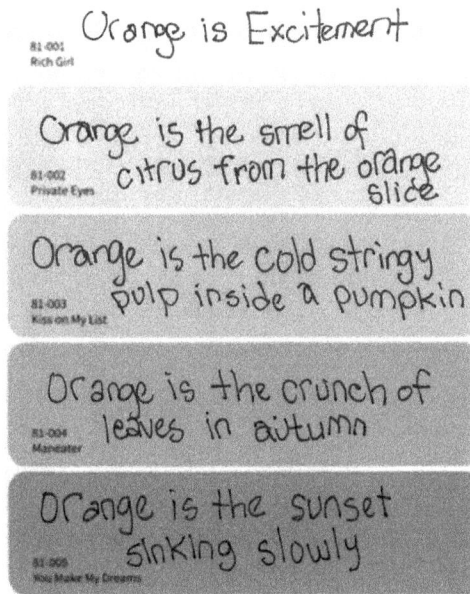

Orange is Excitement

Orange is the smell of citrus from the orange slice

Orange is the cold stringy pulp inside a pumpkin

Orange is the crunch of leaves in autumn

Orange is the sunset sinking slowly

Fact Pocket Poetry

In truth, poetry is poetry. It cannot be classified as fiction or nonfiction. However, poetry can be about anything, including the natural world, and it can bring science and social studies to life for young children. Teaching your students to weave facts into poetry is a wonderful way to combine nonfiction content with different poetic structures and techniques. I recommend including these lessons after students have learned and developed some background knowledge on whatever topic you may be teaching —from insects, to seasons, to weather. Linking the subjects you are already focusing on in Science, Social Studies, and Math with poetry reinforces to students that poetry is everywhere. Once students have learned the structure of different poems and gathered enough facts from their fact pocket and other resources, the possibilities for fact-pocket poetry are endless!

There are a number of exceptional children's poets who masterfully weave information into lyrical, visual, creative poems. Douglas Florian (my personal favorite!), Joyce Sidman, Marilyn Singer, and Irene Latham have all written numerous nonfiction poetry books for children. Bringing these books into your classroom and sharing poems by these poets through daily read-alouds will model to your students that poems not only entertain and inspire us, but can also teach us.

I Like… Poems

"I Like Bugs" by Margaret Wise Brown is my go-to poem to introduce students to nonfiction poetry. Even the youngest poets can quickly catch on to the simple structure and repeating pattern, and many have been known to continue using it independently and write their own I Like… poems.

- Copy the poem "I Like Bugs" by Margaret Wise Brown on chart paper or project it on the interactive whiteboard. This poem can be found in book form, or you can access it online or on YouTube.
- Read the poem aloud, then invite students to read along with you.
- Review the 3 R's of poetry and invite students to help you identify them in the poem. Read the poem and clap the rhythm.
- Copy this cloze poem onto chart paper:

I Like _____ (title)

I like _____
Any kind of _____
_____ _____,
_____ _____,
Any kind of _____

A _____ _____
A _____ _____
_____ _____
_____, _____
Any kind of _____.
I like _____!

- Tell students that you have borrowed the pattern of the poem but that you are going to choose a different topic. Tell the students you want to include real facts in your poem so you are going to find your topic in the fact pocket in your brain.
- Model a write-aloud, filling in the blanks and talking through your word choices. (I recommend not trying to rhyme this poem.)

I Like Bears by A. Gear

I like bears.
Any kind of bears!
Grizzly bears,
Polar bears,
Any kind of bear!

A bear eating berries
A bear catching salmon
Brown bears,
Black bears,

Any kind of bear.
I like bears!

- Pass out the I Like… template on page 143. Depending on what you are focusing on in your content areas, you could link the poem to what your class is studying. Students may need to do some research to gather a few facts to include in their poem if their fact pocket is missing a few facts!

STUDENT SAMPLE POEMS: I LIKE…

"Spiders" Grade 2
"Slugs" Grade 3

I Like Spiders By Mattius

I like spiders
Any kind of spiders!
Wolf spider, widow spider
Any kind of spider.

A spider making silk
A spider laying eggs.
Crab spiders
Bog spiders
Any kind of spider.
I like spiders!

I Like Slugs by Mackenzie

I like slugs
Any kind of slug!
Garden slugs, banana slug,
Any kind of slug.

A slug making mucus.
A slug sensing surroundings.
Invertebrate slug,
Omnivore slug
Any kind of slug.
I like slugs!

Many students are drawn to this poetry pattern and often begin using it independently during brain-pocket writing. I have had students write I Like… Poems about everything from airplanes to nail polish!

Who Am I? Poem

Who Am I? or Riddle Poems encourage students to use language to present a common thing in an unfamiliar way, providing clues and asking their readers to guess what it is. I love teaching this kind of poem; children take to it naturally and love trying to guess each other's riddles. Central to these poems is the use of poetic language: good riddles rely on creative use of metaphor, simile, and imagery. Students are more successful with these poems if they have already been introduced and have had practice in some of the poetic technique lessons (see pages 37–50).

Topic: Animal or object
Structure: Riddle poem
Target: Metaphor (see page 39), simile (see page 37), descriptive imagery
Anchor Poem: "A Small Green Riddle" by Joyce Sidman
Anchor Books:
Davies, Lynn. *So Imagine Me: Nature Riddles in Poetry*
Sidman, Joyce. *Song of the Water Boatman*

- Write this verse on the whiteboard or a shared screen.

    You can open but can't come in.
    I have space, but no room,
    I have keys, but open no lock.
    I have a memory, but do not remember
    What am I?

Answer: a computer

- Read it aloud and invite students to guess the answer.
- Tell students that this is a riddle. Explain that a riddle is written as a collection of clues that form a puzzle to be solved. A *riddle rhyme* is a riddle that is written in the form of a poem. Explain that riddle poems often use poetry techniques, such as personification, metaphor and similes. Ask them if they notice any techniques in the computer riddle (*personification: the computer is talking*).

See page 44 for the lesson on Personification; page 37 for the lesson on Simile.

- Read the poem "A Small Green Riddle" by Joyce Sidman (available on YouTube) from the book *Song of the Water Boatman*. Discuss the clues and poetry techniques (*personification, simile*). Ask students if they know the answer to the riddle. (The answer is Duckweed, but likely nobody will know the answer! I still encourage them to try to guess; most at least conclude it's some kind of plant.)

- Continue the lesson:

   Writers, today we are going to write a riddle poem. The trick to writing a riddle poem is that you have to start with the answer and then work backwards.

- Share the tips for writing a Riddle Poem:

   - Don't use the exact topic word in your riddle or you will give it away!
   - Try not to use more than 5 or 6 lines.
   - It doesn't have to rhyme, but it can if you like.
   - Try to include a simile, personification, or alliteration.
   - End with the line *What am I?* or *Who am I?*

- Continue the lesson:

   Animals are a good topics, but it's best to choose an animal or insect that is a little unusual. I think I'll choose a sloth. First, we will need to brainstorm some interesting facts about sloths. Who can help me?

Record facts about the sloth:

   Lives in trees
   Sleeps a lot
   Shaggy grey fur, flat face
   Hangs upside down
   Long sharp claws
   Long arms
   Two toes or three toes

- Continue the lesson:

   Next, I need to imagine I am a sloth. I'm going to try to describe myself without giving away too many clues. I might include what I look like, what I can do, what my unique characteristics are, and maybe where you would find me. I don't want to make it too easy or too hard for my reader to guess. I am also going think of creative descriptions.

- Model a write-aloud of your poem, modeling how to turn the facts into clues and how to write them in the voice of the sloth. Try to group your sentences into short stanzas.

   I live in a tree with my eyes closed. (eyes closed *instead of* sleepy)
   I'm scraggy and grey, but not very old. (*describing the fur, tried to rhyme* closed-old)

   I have long arms but I'm not an ape.
   I am slow like a turtle and hard to wake (*simile; rhyme with* "ape")

   I can count to two or three on my toes. (*sloths have either 2 or 3 toes*)

Nails help me hang upside down, I suppose. (*sloths have long nails but readers might think it was the other kind of nail; tried to rhyme with toes*)

Who am I?

- Pass out the Riddle Poem Planning Page on page 144. Encourage students to choose an animal or insect they know some facts about but possibly not one that is well known.

STUDENT SAMPLE POEM: RIDDLE POEM

Grade 5
(Answer: tortoise)

Who am I?

I float along in a watery place
Bask in the sun, dig sand in my space.

I swim along with my webbed feet
My flippers help me find a treat.

You can see my home but you can't come in.
I'm older than your great Uncle Jim.

When I am scared I hide my head
But not under a pillow or under a bed.

Who am I?

by Ruby

Animal Acrostic Poem

Topic: An animal (or any topic the students might be researching)
Structure: Acrostic poem (see page 67)
Target: facts and poetic devices (simile, alliteration, repetition, personification; see pages 37, 45, 43, and 41)
Anchor Books
Hummon, David. *Animal Acrostics*
Shaneyfelt, Stacy. *A Science and Poetic Safari: Animal Acrostic Poems*

At one point in a child's education, they are likely to be assigned some kind of research report. Among the most frequently assigned reports are the ever-popular animal reports! (I used to do Arctic Animal research reports with my Grade 4 students every year!) Students choose an animal and research facts about appearance, habitat, diet, enemies, and life cycles. Once the research is complete, reports are written and presented. I'm a big fan of not making more work for myself or my students, so why not use the information they have already gathered about their animal (or insect, plant, or country) and create a poem with it? An acrostic poem provides just enough structure, while allowing students to include facts and poetic devices. If you have not yet introduced acrostic poetry to your students, I recommend doing so before this lesson (see lesson on page 67).

- Explain to students that sometimes, poets like to write poems that include facts and information about a topic. Sometimes they use facts stored in their fact pocket, other times they need to gather facts by researching their topic.
- Remind students that they have been researching animals (plants, insect, countries, habitats) and that they have gathered some interesting facts about their research topics. Explain that they will be using some of those facts to write a poem.

- Review the structure of an acrostic poem (see lesson on page 67). Discuss the difference between a single-scoop acrostic poem and a triple-scoop one.

  > Single-scoop: only one word per letter per line
  > Triple-scoop: longer phrases, can continue on two lines, includes poetic devices

- Show an example of a single-scoop acrostic about a panda:

  > **P**layful
  > **A**nimal
  > **N**ice
  > **D**ances
  > **A**wesome.

  Ask students why it might be a single-scoop acrostic (*words aren't really describing the panda; no real facts; "nice" and "awesome" are single-scoop words*).

- Show example of a triple-scoop acrostic about a panda:

  > **P**aws pointed inward
  > **A**s it plods along.
  > **N**octurnal eyes glow as it searches through darkness.
  > **D**aytime dozer
  > **A** misty mountain dweller.

For more great examples of triple-scoop animal acrostics, visit: https://slidetodoc.com/acrostic-poems-by-mrs-davis-first-grade-panda/

- Discuss why this acrostic is much better. (*First line flows into the second line; includes many panda facts; includes alliteration "misty mountain," "paws pointed," "daytime dozer"*)
- Share some poems from either of the recommended anchor books. It's important for students to see these poems, as well as listen to them, if possible.
- Students can use the Acrostic Poem template on page 87 and the What's the Scoop? Acrostic Poems template on page 88 when writing their animal poems.

STUDENT SAMPLE POEM: ANIMAL ACROSTIC

Grade 4

SLOTH

Sluggish and sleepy 22 hours a day (yawn!)
Lives in the treetops of Central America (so high!)
Only goes to the bathroom once a week (wow!)
There algea green fur camoflagshes (can't see me!)
Hiss and claw - the big cats and hawks are here
(can you say enime?)

Arjun

Content List Poem

While information from our fact pockets and other resources can be integrated into many of the poetic structures, I have found the structure of list poetry one of the most accessible and versatile. Remember—poems hide! So, whether you are teaching explorers, seasonal changes, immigration, life cycles, weather, or habitats, there is a list poem just waiting to be discovered!

- Project or copy "Clouds" by Douglas Florian poem on chart paper. Read it aloud, then ask students to read it with you.
- Discuss the 3 R's. (*It has rhyme and rhythm, but no repetition.*)
- Review the features of a list poem:

  - a list of words or phrases connected to a topic
  - sometimes tells a story
  - usually only two words per line
  - last words on each line usually have the same ending: *-er* or *-ing*

- Invite the class to help you write a list poem about the wind. Write the title at the top of a T-chart on chart paper or the whiteboard. On the left side of the chart, begin to list objects that wind can blow: *windows, doors, hair, grass, leaves,* etc. Invite students to help you add to the list.
- On the right side of the chart, beside each word, write a verb connected to the object. What does the wind do to the objects? (*windows shake, hair wrecks, grass rustles*)
- Explain that because you want the second word in each line to have the same ending, you are going to add *-er* to the end of each verb.

What does the wind blow?	What does the wind do?
Hair	wrecker
Branch	cracker
Umbrella	breaker
Balloon	stealer
Kite	blower
Windmill	spinner
Dandelion	spreader
Fire	shifter
Dress	whisperer
Grass	dancer
Leaf	mover
Paper	popper
Bubble	

- When you have finished brainstorming, read the poem aloud, beginning with the title "Wind."
- Invite students to write their own list poem on a different type of weather, including extreme weather (e.g., snow, rain, fog, hail, sun, thunderstorm, tornado, tsunami) using the two-column List Poem template on page 89.

Topic: Any topic in Social Studies or Science

Structure: List poem (see page 69)

Target: The 3 R's: rhyme is optional (see page 14)

Anchor Poem: "Clouds" by Douglas Florian

Anchor Books:

Heard, Georgia. *Falling Down the Page*

Salas, Laura Purdie. *A Leaf Can Be…*

See page 69 for the lesson on List Poems.

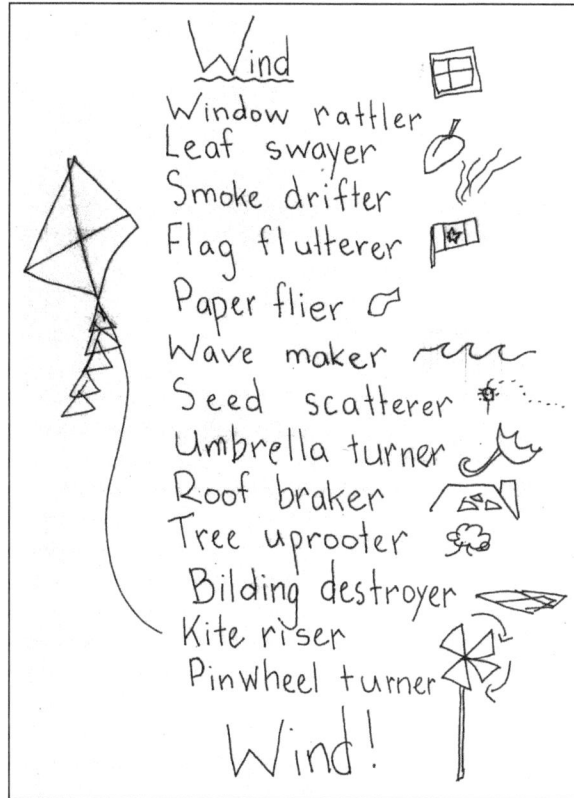

Wind
Window rattler
Leaf swayer
Smoke drifter
Flag flutterer
Paper flier
Wave maker
Seed scatterer
Umbrella turner
Roof braker
Tree uprooter
Bilding destroyer
Kite riser
Pinwheel turner
Wind!

EXTENSION

The list poem format works well for writing about many topics in science and social studies. Students can choose something they are learning about and brainstorm facts connected to it. Depending on the topic, students can sequence their ideas to tell a story. See student samples below: "Rainforest," by a Grade 5 student, includes issues affecting the ecosystem.

STUDENT SAMPLE POEMS: CONTENT LIST POEMS

Rainforest by Kali	**Explorers**	**Winter** by Jessie
Canopy covering	Sails rising	Temperature dropping
Rain falling	Ship sailing	Snow falling
Sun shining	Sailors working	Mittens wearing
Leaves falling	Captain calling	Snowball rolling
Organisms growing	Telescopes searching	Snowman making
Forest floor	Waves crashing	Snowball throwing
decomposing	Compass spinning	Snowboots crunching
Soil fertilizing	Map making	Cars slipping
Animals surviving	Land discovering	Slush spraying
Animals thriving	Anchor dropping	Angel arms swishing
Loggers cutting	Native greeting	Icicles dripping
Animals dying.	Goods trading	Kids laughing
	Friends making	Winter.

I Am… Personification Poem

Old Elm Speaks: Tree Poems can be found as a read aloud on YouTube. The first poem in the book, "Oak's Introduction," is written in the voice of the tree and makes a great anchor for this lesson.

See page 41 for the lesson on Personification.

One of the things I enjoy about nonfiction, or fact-pocket, poetry is how writers can transform facts in creative ways using a wide variety of poetic structure and techniques. I Am … poems do just that; they personify content topics to create an informative, innovative poem. Topics that work well for these personification poems are scientific topics that feature movement or change: matter, bodies of water, body systems, ecosystems, the water cycle, human body systems, any life cycle; historical events, objects, landmarks, or structures in social studies, such as Indigenous artifacts (totem pole, button blanket), pyramids, sphinx, Stonehenge, the Eiffel Tower, The Great Wall of China.

- Review personification: when a poet gives human character traits (movement, voice, feelings) to a non-human object.
- Explain that students will be writing a poem based on a science or social studies topic they have been learning about. What will make this poem interesting is that they will be taking the topic and personifying it; i.e., writing about it as if it were human, as if it were talking.
- Copy "Oak's Introduction" onto chart paper. Read it aloud and ask students who is talking in the poem (*the tree*). Discuss how the poet is using personification and is giving the tree a voice and feelings.
- Explain that you will be showing how to write a poem with this technique, using the topic of a river. Brainstorm some attributes of a river: helps move water to the sea, provides energy for hydro, provides nutrients for animals and fish, provides transport. Try to narrow it down to four or five big ideas.
- Model, using a write-aloud, sharing your ideas as you record the poem. Begin each stanza with "I am…" (see poem below)

I Am a River

I am a river of travel
Flowing and carrying
Water to the sea

I am a river of nutrients
Growing and feeding
Animals and birds

I am a river of energy
Powering and strengthening
Hydro stations and power plants

I am a river of transport
Travelling and exploring
New worlds and new adventures.

I am a river.

- Discuss how you wrote the poem in the river's voice; the pattern and repetition of the poem; and how each stanza focuses on one of the big ideas.
- Invite students to find a topic from their fact pocket that they have been learning about, either at school or at home. Explain that they will need to know at least four facts about their topic in order to write their poem. Depending on your grade, you may choose to brainstorm the big ideas as a class.

- Once the facts are gathered, students can begin to write their poems. Each big idea or fact will be a new stanza. Encourage students to write in first person ("I") and to try to include the voice of the object, not just the facts. Remind them of poetic devices they can include, in particular repetition and alliteration.

STUDENT SAMPLE POEMS: I AM...

"You're Welcome" Grade 7
"Don't Look" Grade 3

You're Welcome by Jasmeet

I am your blood
Pumping and flowing
Oxygen and nutrients
Into your cells.
You're welcome.

I am your blood
Pushing carbon dioxide out
Through other organs.
Just say no to waste.
You're welcome.

I am your blood
Regulating your temperature
And fighting infections
Just say no to Covid
You're welcome.

I am your blood
Clotting and forming clots
So you don't bleed out
All over the place.
You're welcome.

I am your blood.

Don't Look! by Adrianna

I am an egg.
I sit on a leaf
with my brothers and sisters.

I am a larva.
I munch on leaves all day.
I grow and shed my skin.

I am a pupa.
I hide away inside the chrysalis.
Don't look! I'm changing!

I am an adult butterfly
my soft wings unfold
And I am beautiful.

I am a butterfly.

Antonym Diamante for Comparing

Comparative writing involves being able to identify and articulate the similarities and differences between two topics. In my book *Powerful Writing Structures*, I outline the structure and language associated with this form of writing and how well it can be linked to writing in the content areas linked to Social Studies and Science topics:

Comparing countries (e.g., Canada and Japan)
Comparing animals (e.g., crocodile and alligator)
Comparing biomes/habitats (e.g., tropical rainforest and temperate rainforest)
Comparing body systems (e.g., respiratory system and digestive system)
Comparing cultural celebrations (e.g., Lunar New Year and Diwali)
Comparing weather (e.g., tornados and cyclones)
Comparing seasons (e.g., spring and fall)
Comparing indigenous groups (e.g., Haida and Inuit)
Comparing regions of Canada (e.g., West Coast and Prairies)
Comparing forms of government (e.g., democracy and dictatorship)

Topic: any two topics in Social Studies and Science you can compare
Structure: Antonym diamante (see page 66)
Target: Facts; triple-scoop words; nouns, verbs, and adjectives
Anchor Books:
Pallotta, Jerry. Who Would Win series
Strack, Emma. *What's the Difference?: 40+ Pairs of the Seemingly Similar*

See page 66 for the lesson on the Antonym Diamante.

Diamante poems are great for integrating a lesson on parts of speech: nouns, verbs, and adjectives!

Diamante is a structure of poetry originating in Italy. It consists of seven lines written about a topic in the shape of a diamond (see lesson on page 63). There are two different types of diamante poems: synonym and antonym. For an antonym diamante, the poet needs to choose two nouns that are opposite; e.g., sun–moon, pencil–eraser, dog–cat, fairy–witch, desert–rainforest, Superman–Spiderman. Antonym diamantes can, of course, be written about anything, but a popular way of using them is to compare and contrast two subjects students are learning about in Social Studies or Science.

- Draw a Venn diagram on the board or chart paper. Write the words *Cat* and *Rabbit* on either side of the Venn. Tell students they are going to be comparing these two animals by thinking about how they are the same and how they are different from each other.
- Invite students to spend two minutes with a partner describing how both these animals are the same (*pets, mammals, fur, whiskers, companions*) and how they are different (*meow/no sound, walks/hops, Halloween/Easter, long tail/short tail, small ears/big ears*). Invite students to share their ideas while you record them in the centre of the Venn.
- Explain that you are going to show them how to use the information from the Venn to write a compare and contrast poem called an antonym (opposite) diamante. Remind students of the features of a diamante: 7 lines long; in the shape of a diamond; includes nouns, adjectives and verbs.
- Lightly draw a diamond shape on the board or on chart paper. Write the word *Cat* inside at the top of the diamond and *Rabbit* at the bottom. Explain that this poem will start by describing the cat and end with describing the rabbit. The middle line of the poem is the "switch-over" line, where the first two words are about the first subject and the second two words switch to the second.
- Ask students for two adjectives to describe a cat, followed by three verbs. Record those on the next two lines.
- Continue the write-aloud and complete the poem on the chart stand or board:

Cat
independent, sleek
purring, scratching, licking
fur, claws, whiskers, bob-tail
hopping, jumping, chewing
fluffy, quiet
Rabbit

- Depending on the subject you are focusing on in Science or Social Studies, diamante poems could be used for comparing two related topics.

Tundra
Cold, treeless
freezing, melting, disappearing
North, Arctic, Africa, Middle East
scorching, drying, adapting
sand, sun
Desert

Democracy
Fair, free
electing, voting, voicing
people, rights, power, rules
forcing, suppressing, persecuting
unfair, cruel
Dictatorship

Imagination Pocket Poems

Poems that emerge from our imagination are filled with wonder and creativity. When a child is free to write about superheroes, unicorns, dragons, Minecraft, and glitter slime that talks, their poetic self emerges! When it comes to imagination, a few favorite poets come to mind: Shel Silverstein, Jack Prelutsky, Kenn Nesbitt, and Michael Rosen. Using these poets as mentors can inspire our students to stretch their imagination, take risks, and share a little of their individuality. While other poems are more structured, I encourage my students to do more free-verse writing when we are sourcing out of our imagination pocket. By this time, they have enough knowledge about poetry structure and techniques that I allow some free writing on topics of their choice.

ANCHOR BOOKS FOR IMAGINATION POCKET POETRY

Hopkins, Lee Bennett. *I Am Someone Else: Poems About Pretending*

Kuskin, Karla. *Dogs and Dragons, Trees and Dreams*

Topic: Pretending to be something else
Structure: Stanza format
Target: First-person point of view, repetition (see page 43)
Anchor Poem: "If I Were a..." by Karla Kuskin

If I Were... Poem

Poems are wonderful places for children to pretend, to dream, and to imagine. Playing with reality, ideas, and language can all be done in one place! Karla Kuskin's "If I Were A..." is a wonderful mentor poem for this lesson, not only because it models stretching our imagination, but it includes the 3 R's (rhyme, repetition, and rhythm) and a simple pattern the students can use for writing their own pretending poem.

- Write the poem on chart paper:

  If I Were a... by A. Gear (based on the poem *If I Were a...* by Karla Kuskin)

  If I were a bee,
  I would buzz like a bee
  With a high little hum
  I would zip around free.
  I would work in my hive
  Until way past five
  Being a bee.

  If I were a whale
  I would swim like a whale
  Majestically swimming
  And slapping my tail.
  Just blowing my spout
  And looking for trout
  Being a whale.

  If I were I daisy
  I'd stand in the grass
  Growing up proudly
  As children run past.
  I'd sway in the breeze
  Make friends with the bees
  Being a daisy.

  If I were a pizza,
  I'd sit on a plate
  And think of my toppings
  Until someone ate
  Me.
  No more pizza.
  No more poem.

- Read aloud "If I Were a..." by Karla Kuskin or my adaptation of the poem above. Invite students to listen and identify rhyming words, repetition, and rhythm.
- Ask students what the poem is about (*pretending, imagining, point of view*). Ask students if they ever go into their imagination pocket and pretend to be someone or something else.
- Ask students to think about an animal, insect, plant, object, person they would like to pretend to be. Invite them to close their eyes and quietly pretend they have transformed into the imaginary creature or object. Ask them: *What are you? What do you look like? What can you do? What are your special abilities? What do you like doing?*
- Model your thinking:

  I'm going to pretend that I'm a pencil because I think it would be fun to write for someone. So I am long, thin and orange. I have lead inside me and an eraser on my end. I live in desks, drawers, and people's purses. I write letters, words, and numbers, and I draw. I'm good at writing and I like to help people tell stories and poems.

- Invite students to turn and talk to a partner, describing themselves as their imaginary object or animal.
- Pass out the If I Were… Poem Planning Page on page 146. Use it to model how to record your ideas on the page. Students can complete their own page.
- Model how you might take the ideas from the planning page and write a poem:

> If I were a pencil,
> I would write like a pencil,
> Quietly scratching.
> I'd move across your page
> With my pointy lead tip
> Helping you write poems
> If I were a pencil.

- Discuss how you started and ended the poem with the same line. Point out how you tried to describe an action in detail, and included some sensory words: *quietly scratching, pointy*.
- Students can use the If I Were… template on page 147 to write their poem, if they wish.

STUDENT SAMPLE POEMS: IF I WERE…

Grade 4

If I Were Spiderman
If I were Spiderman
I'd wall crawl like Spiderman
Rapidly flexing
My superpowrs all over New York
I'd rescue the good guys
and zap the bad guys
If I were Spiderman.
By Jasper

If I Were A Unicorn by Riley

If I were a unicorn
I would fly like a unicorn
Happily jumping
On clouds with my friends.
I'd slide down a rainbow
Shooting magical powers from my horn
If I were a unicorn.

Topic: Imaginary creatures
Structure: Free verse (see page 80) or rhyming stanzas
Target: Descriptive details; poetry elements: repetition (see page 43), alliteration (see page 45), rhyme (see page 49)
Anchor Poems:
"The Wendigo" by Ogden Nash
"Jabberwocky" by Lewis Carroll
"Me" by Karla Kuskin
"Glurp, the Purple Alien" by Kenn Nesbitt
Anchor Books:
Zemach, Harve. *The Judge: An Untrue Tale*
Morris, Jackie. *Tell Me A Dragon*

Imaginary Creature Poem

One of my favorite visualizing lessons from *Reading Power* is reading Lewis Carroll's classic poem "Jabberwocky" and inviting students to visualize and draw a scene from the poem (*Reading Power*, page 76). This poem is full of imaginary words and creatures, and, over the years, I have watched students delight in their detailed drawings of the Tumtum tree, the juvious Bandersnatch, or the dreaded Jabberwocky. The reader requires no pictures in order to imagine the fearful creature Carroll created. This lesson invites students to create their own imaginary creature and write a poem with enough detail that the reader can visualize it.

- Explain to students that you are going to read a poem about an imaginary creature, but you are not going to show them a picture yet because you want them to visualize and imagine what the creature looks like.
- Read aloud any of the recommended poems or books and invite students to visualize. I often read the poem twice so that they can mentally add more details to their visual image.

- Invite students to describe the creature they "saw" to a partner. An option, depending on your time, is to invite students to sketch the imaginary creature and compare their drawing with a partner's.
- Discuss the 3 R's (rhyme, repetition, rhythm).
- Discuss what the poet did to help us visualize (*triple-scoop words, sensory details, descriptive words, colors, size,* etc.)
- Tell students that they are going to be writing poems about an imaginary creature. First, they need to go into their imagination pocket to find their creature. Remind students that, while the creatures from the poems were scary, their imaginary creature can be silly or strange or funny.
- Teacher Model:

> *My imaginary creature is called a Bee Bop. It's got purple hair and green eyes that kind of pop out of its head. It's got blue hair and blue teeth, and this kind of zig-zag tail—and the weird part is that the tail can scream! It has a really long tongue that can touch the ground. The Bee Bop eats bumble bees and burps a lot.*

- Create a chart and add your ideas as you describe your creature:

My creature is a Bee Bop	Appearance • purple hair • green eyes • blue teeth • zig-zag tail • long tongue • green
Eats and drinks • bumble bees • rusty keys	Sounds and smells • tail screams • burps
My creature can (Special features or abilities) • scream from its tail	My creature is (personality) • shy • afraid of grass

- Give students a few moments to think and then invite them to describe their imaginary creature to a partner. Encourage them to visualize details, such as hair, eyes, body, special features, what it likes to eat, what it likes to do, etc.
- Provide the Imaginary Creature Planning Page on page 148 to record some of their ideas. Students can draw their creature and label their drawing, or they can write on their plan.
- When students have complete their plans, model using your ideas to write a poem.

My Bee-Bop by A. Gear

My Bee-Bop has long purple hair
And eyes that pop out green
Its hair is blue
Its teeth are too
Its zig-zag tail can scream

My Bee-Bop has a crooked nose
Its tongue can touch the ground
It likes to sleep
Beneath my feet
It makes a funny sound

My Bee-Bop is afraid of grass
And burps when music plays
Eats rusty keys
And bumble bees
But I want it to stay.

- Tell students they can write a poem that has rhyming words and stanzas or use free-verse style. Remind them that a poem must have at least one of the 3 R's —rhyme, repetition, or rhythm—and it needs to look like a poem, with shorter lines and white spaces. Encourage students to include triple-scoop words and similes. Afterwards, students can illustrate their poem.

STUDENT SAMPLE POEM: IMAGINARY CREATURE

Grade 3

Spider Ghost

The Spider Ghost is comig hear
Watch out! Watch out!
It Has 65 legs!
And 34 arms!
And spits out venom from its but
Nasty!

The Spider Ghost is coming near
Watch out! Watch out!
you Better Run faaaaast!
His black tung
Can wrap around you
And squeez you
Like a King cobra
Til your eyes pop out!
Nasty!

Nathan

Children's poet Kenn Nesbitt has an amazing website with many of his poems in text and audio form. He has an entire page dedicated to imaginary poems that I highly recommend for inspiring imaginary topics for your students' poems. https://www.poetry4kids.com/topic/imaginary/

Topic: How-to instructions
Structure: List poem (see page 69)
Target: Alliteration (see page 45)
Anchor Books:
Clibbon, Lucy and Meg. Imagine You're A… (series)
Hill, Susanna Leonard. *When Your Llama Needs a Haircut*
Janeczko, Paul B. *The Proper Way to Meet a Hedgehog and Other How-To Poems*
Pilutti, Deb. *Ten Steps to Flying Like a Superhero*
Wallace, Adam. How to Catch A… (series)

How to Be… Poem

I first developed the How to Be… idea in my *Nonfiction Writing Power* book for teaching instructional writing. Once I started realizing the number of possibilities in using the frame in the content areas, I couldn't stop! Everything from How to Be an Explorer to How to Be an Orca Whale to How to Celebrate Diwali to How to Have a Smudging Ceremony. Once students know the writing structure and language, it is easy to weave in the content. While our fact pockets, along with other resources, are often our source when incorporating how-to into the content areas, the concept and format can be easily adapted to creating how-to poems based on imaginary characters. Students love the freedom to choose any imaginary character they like, including characters from video games (yes, video games!).

- Tell students that they are going to be using their imagination pocket to help them with today's poem.
- Write *How To* on the board or chart stand. Ask them what connection they make to the words. (*instructions on how to do something, make something*, etc.)
- Explain that, most often, instructions are written to help someone know exactly how to do real activities, such as fix a bike, make cookies, do a worksheet; therefore, most writers would use their fact pockets to write them. But this time, students will be using their imagination pockets to write some imaginary how-to poems.
- Share one or more of the anchor books or poems with the class. Discuss how the writer was using their imagination to create the instructions on how to be or how to do something imaginary.
- Brainstorm some imaginary people or creatures that could be used as the topic of their How To Be… poem:

a mermaid	Spiderman, Batman (any super hero)
a fairy	
a pirate	Dr. Doom, She-Hulk, Gutbomb, Big Chuggas (any video game characters)
a dragon	
a unicorn	
a Lego figure	Fairy Tale characters
Paw Patrol characters	Disney characters
Peppa Pig	

- Tell students that it is important to choose a character that they know quite a bit about, including what they look like (appearance, clothing, etc.), their special features or abilities (can fly, disappear, become invisible), and their personality (brave, shy, athletic)
- Model brainstorming onto a chart or table. I used the character Little Red Riding Hood for my example.

What does your character look like? (include clothing)	**What special abilities does your character have? What special things can your character do?**
Red cape with a hood Basket of food	No special abilities She saves her grandmother
What is your character's personality?	**Draw a picture of your character here:**
Kind Brave Curious Smart	

- Invite students to share their character with a partner and describe the character in detail.
- Pass out the How to Be an Imaginary Character Planning Page on page 149. Students can record their ideas on the page and draw a picture of their character.
- When students have completed their planning page, model how to use the facts to create an imaginary How to Be… poem.

How to Be Little Red Riding Hood

Be a little girl
Always wear a red cape
Carry a basket to Granny's house
Through the woods
Through the woods.

Go inside
See a strange person in bed
Ask curious questions
Be cautious and brave then
SCREAM!

Help save your grandmother!
Great job, Little Red!

- Discuss how you broke the poem into stanzas and tried to include some repetition (*Through the woods*) and alliteration (*curious questions*). Tell them you also added an ending.

STUDENT SAMPLE POEMS: HOW TO BE

"Lego Man" Grade 4

How to Be a Cool Lego Man

Be real smart but real cool
Have yellow skin
Wear a plastic wig
Have arms and legs that click
Never change your smile
Have weird hands and only 2 fingrs
Have square feet
Hang out in any lego land you want
Be a cool Lego man.
Yah, you are a Cool Lego Man!

By Roy

How to Be a Fairy by Stella

Be very small
Have wings and fly
Sparkle and shine
Carry a wand
Have bells
Grant wishes
Always be kind to everyone
Sleep in a flower
Make friends with the bees
Sprinkle fairy dust everywhere
Fairy dust everywhere.
Fairy dust makes everything better.

Introduce "Tip" words to include in how-to poems: *always…, never…, try to…, remember to…*

Assessing Poetry

"Do you have a rubric for that?" I'm often faced with this question during workshops and teacher training. Teachers want to know how to assess what they are teaching—I understand that. And while it is helpful for us to have a breakdown of what we should be looking for in the poetry our students are writing in the form of an assessment rubric, it somehow doesn't feel right to compress a poem into a grid. How does one truly assess a poem when it is so subjective? Surely, meaning and feeling should factor in alongside structure and spelling, but how do you assess a feeling? As I have said throughout this book, a poem is more than the sum of its parts. A poem can be neat, include all the necessary structure, poetic devices, formatting, and conventions; however, if it does not say something old in a new way, move me, surprise me, make me smile, tear up, or give me shivers, it's not a perfect poem.

When assessing poems with our students, we can go through our editing checklists and rubrics. But ultimately, if we want our students to improve their poetry skills, they need to be part of the assessment process and to learn to identify the aspects of poetry that really matter. What matters most is not the way the poem looks, but the way it sounds and the way it makes a reader feel. That's what we should be focusing on when we assess poetry. I recommend providing students with a self-reflection that invites them to value the inside of the poem as well as the outside.

Does your poem look like a poem? (shorter lines, more white spaces, line breaks between stanzas)
Does your poem sound like a poem? Include the 3 R's (rhyme, rhythm, repetition)
Does your poem sound like you? Can you hear your voice when you read it out loud?
Does your poem include some poetic devices? (simile, alliteration, personification)
Does your poem say something old in a new or surprising way?
Does your poem give you a feeling without saying the feeling?
Does it give your reader something to think about?
Are you proud of your poem?

Poetry Assessment Rubrics

Assessment rubrics help us guide our instruction, be responsive, look for gaps, and identify the specific areas of learning we need to target. Below is a rubric that could help in this process. While it is not grade-specific, it provides you with a sense of what to look for when evaluating your students' poetry. I recommend using this when assessing a collection of poems by the same student, rather than for individual, isolated poems.

POETRY	Description	Emerging	Beginning	Developing	Extending
Meaning	**Poem is meaningful:** makes sense; is easy to follow, interesting, original; possibly tells a story				
Style	**Poem has style:** is engaging, unique; includes effective word choice, descriptive language, use of the 3 R's; poetic devices attempted (similes, personification, alliteration, etc.); sounds like a poem				
Form	**Poem is structured:** follows the specific poetic structure as modeled by the teacher; is well-developed, is organized in stanzas (if applicable), looks like a poem				
Feeling	**Poem has feeling:** says something old in a new way, has impact on the reader, lingers.				
Conventions	**Poem is clear:** accurate spelling of high-frequency words; errors do not interfere with meaning; poetry spacing/formatting used, "looks" like a poem (shorter lines, more white spaces)				

I Am From...

Name: _____

I am from _____
(describe your home on the outside)

From _____
(decorations or special objects inside)

I am from _____
(plants that grow near or in your house)

I am from _____
(activities your family does outside)

From _____
(activities your family does inside)

I am from _____
(two favorite family foods or meals)

From _____
(more special foods or drinks)

I am from _____
(names of pet or pets if you have them)

From _____
(names of 3 special toys or stuffies)

I am from _____
(3 family celebrations)

I am from _____
(2 special objects in your house)

From _____
(2 more objects)

I am from _____
(family country of origin, cultures)

From _____
(church or religion)

I am from _____
(2 family traits)

I am from _____
(2 feelings connected to your family)

Pembroke Publishers © 2021 *Powerful Poetry* by Adrienne Gear ISBN 978-1-55138-352-1

I'm Talking Family Member (Primary)

Name: _____

I'm Talking _____!

By _____

I'm talking _____!

I'm talking _____ (name you call your _____)

I'm talking _____ , _____

(2 character traits)

I'm talking _____ , _____ , _____

(3 jobs your _____ does)

I'm talking _____ , _____ , _____ ,

_____ ,

(4 triple-scoop describing words)

I'm talking _____

(1 feeling word)

I'm talking _____ !

Pembroke Publishers © 2021 *Powerful Poetry* by Adrienne Gear ISBN 978-1-55138-352-1

Family Metaphor Planning Page

Name: _____

Topic: _____

1. Choose a topic that has different topics connected to it; for example, Weather.

2. List the subtopics as items in column 1: e.g., sunshine, lightning, snow, hail, rainbow, tornado.

3. Describe the qualities of each item.

4. Match each item to a member of your family. Don't forget to include yourself!

Items	Description	Family Member

When I Was Young Planner

Name: _____

I grew up in _____

List places you remember going to and what you remember about each place.

Place	What you remember seeing, doing, feeling there

Use some of the ideas above to write your free verse poem.

When I was Young in _____ by _____

When I was young in _____

I remember

_____

_____

_____

_____

When I was young in _____

I remember

_____

_____

_____

_____

Feeling Poem

Name: _____

Think of a time in your life when you remember experiencing a big feeling. Describe what happened:

I felt _____ when…

_____

_____

_____

Write your feeling poem without writing the feeling word! Use free verse and try to include simile, repetition, and alliteration.

_____

_____

_____

_____

_____

_____

_____

_____

_____

Gratiku: Gratitude Haiku

Name: _____

I'm grateful for _____.

It's special to me because

_____

_____

_____

Write your Gratiku in the box . Remember to follow the 5-7-5 syllable count and include a word like *thankful* or *grateful* somewhere in your poem. Illustrate your poem.

_____

_____

_____

Apology Poem

Name: _____

Think of a time you did something you needed to apologize for. What did you do?

_____

_____

_____

What did you see, hear, smell, touch, feel when you were doing what you weren't supposed to do?

I saw	I heard	I smelled
_____	_____	_____
_____	_____	_____

I tasted	I felt
_____	_____
_____	_____

This Is Just to Say by _____

_____

_____

_____

_____

_____

_____

_____

Noisy Place Poem Planner

Name: _____

Choose a noisy place for your poem: _____

What objects and sounds do you find in your noisy place?

Object	Sound

Now use your sound words to write your poem that tells a little story about your noisy place.

_____

_____

_____

_____

_____

_____

Six Senses of Color

Name: _____

_____
(your chosen color)

Sights	
Smells	
Sounds	
Tastes	
Feelings (touch)	
Feelings (emotions)	

I Like…

Name: _____

I like _____

I like _____

Any kind of _____

_____   _____,

_____   _____,

Any kind of _____

A _____   _____

A _____   _____

_____   _____,

_____,   _____

Any kind of _____

I like _____

Pembroke Publishers © 2021 *Powerful Poetry* by Adrienne Gear ISBN 978-1-55138-352-1

Riddle Poem Planning Page

Name: _____

My poem is going to be about a _____

Write as many facts as you can about your topic in the box below. Include interesting behaviors or features that make your topic unique.

Choose 3-4 important words and try to find a rhyming word for each.

_____ rhymes with _____

_____ rhymes with _____

_____ rhymes with _____

_____ rhymes with _____

Now imagine you are that animal and you can talk. How would you describe yourself?

I look like _____

I sound like _____

You will find me _____

I have _____ *but* _____

I am _____ *but* _____

I feel _____

Riddle Poem Planning Page (cont'd)

Now you are ready to write your riddle poem! Leave a new clue on each line. Try to rhyme, if you can. Remember NOT to write your answer in the poem. End your poem with *Who Am I?*

If I Were... Poem Planning Page

Name: _____

Choose what you would like to be: (animal, insect, plant, object, person)

_____

Describe yourself:

What do you look like? (hair, eyes, skin)	What special abilities do you have?
What special features do you have? (wings, fire, tail)	**What are you really good at?**
Where do you live?	**Draw a picture**

Pembroke Publishers © 2021 *Powerful Poetry* by Adrienne Gear ISBN 978-1-55138-352-1

If I Were...

I Were a _____

By _____

If I were a _____ ,

I would _____ like a _____ .

_____   _____

_____

I'd _____

_____

If I were a _____ .

Imaginary Creature Planning Page

Name: _____

My imaginary creature is	Appearance
_____ 	_____ _____ _____ _____ _____
Eats and drinks	**Sounds and smells**
_____ _____ _____ _____	_____ _____ _____ _____
Special features or abilities	**My creature is (personality)**
_____ _____ _____ _____	_____ _____ _____ _____

How to Be an Imaginary Character Planning Page

Name: _____

My character's name: _____

My character is from: _____ (movie, video game, TV show, book, etc.)

What does your character look like? (include details of clothing, face, hair, etc.)	**What special abilities does your character have? What special things can your character do?**
_____ _____ _____ _____ _____	_____ _____ _____ _____
What is your character's personality?	**Draw a picture of your character here:**
_____ _____ _____ _____ _____	

Pembroke Publishers © 2021 *Powerful Poetry* by Adrienne Gear ISBN 978-1-55138-352-1

Final Thoughts

"Poems hang out where life is." — Susan Goldsmith
Woolridge (1996, p. 4)

They say things happen for a reason. I realize now that the reason my lessons were cut from my last book was so that I could write this one. And so, I end this book with the same question I started with: Why not poetry? Certainly, when we think about all that we have endured in the last couple of years during this global pandemic, teaching poetry might seem irrelevant. Who has time to teach poetry when we are all just trying to get through the day with our masks on, hands washed, and distances kept? My answer is simple—because poetry matters. Poetry is not merely a subject to teach; it is a gift of words and language brimming with emotion, imagination, creativity, and joy we can give our students. Because now, more than ever, our students need poetry in their lives. They need a way to shape their thoughts and feelings into something other than a five-paragraph essay. Poetry is so much more than the structure or device we often disguise it in. It is the glimpses, memories, images, and the hidden layers of feelings that need a home. Poetry is pleasure; it is fun and playful and transforming; it is rain falling, monsters in my closet, and my best friend moving away. Poetry is laughter, love, hope, and redemption. Poetry is life.

My hope is that you, the educators reading this book, have discovered or reacquainted yourself with this experience of poetry and, in turn, will help your students discover the poems that live inside them so that they may find new ways to look at the world.

> Powerful poems can
> Open eyes, hearts, and minds. No more
> Excuses that time escaped you,
> Teachers.
> Read, write, rejoice, recite…
> Your students are waiting.
>
> — Adrienne Gear

Acknowledgments

Whenever I start writing a new book, "my people" take a step back and watch from afar as I dig deep and cut myself off from much of the everyday. "She's writing again," they say. But seven books in, they have come to understand that, while I may be a little grumpy, forget to cook supper, and lose things in the dryer that aren't even meant to be in there, not writing would be worse. Not writing means that I am cluttered up there in my head, and being cluttered at my age is not a good thing.

And so, they watch from afar and, with love and patience, wait until I transfer my clutter onto the page in some semblance of order. This book was written during a pandemic, when my job and my home were turned completely upside down, not to mention having a very dislocated elbow and shattered toe—so, there's that, too. I started writing this book on January 26, 2021, and pressed Send to my editor on June 1. Fittingly, June 1 is my dad's birthday. He died when I was in my twenties, far too young, but it feels only right that I finished the draft of this book about teaching poetry on his birthday. My dad was a high-school English teacher before he became a principal, and apart from his family and a good Scotch ("a wee dram"), my dad loved words. He gifted this love of words to me and my two sisters. I know he would be proud.

I recently heard Dr. Jody Carrington speak at a virtual conference. She was talking about how important it is to reconnect after the pandemic. One of the ways she suggested was to surround yourself with "your people"—the ones you can sit around with, braless, and share a good story and a good belly laugh. I am blessed to have a circle of braless women with whom I can weep, giggle, and belly laugh at a moment's notice. Thank you to "my people": Cheryl Burian, Kathleen Keeler, Sue Stevenson, Heather Berry, Kimberly Matterson, Kimberly Stacey, Donna Boardman, Katie McCormack, Lisa Wilson, Donna Kozak, Amy Wou, Laura Grills, Mary Cottrell, and Jeanette Mumford.

Special thanks always to my bestie, Cheryl Burian. You stood by me when I wrote poems to boys in university, even though it was a bad idea, and handed me Kleenex when the poems didn't work. This year has been a struggle for us both; having you to cheer me on and cheer me up has kept me in the game. Your now infamous text after Amanda Gorman's performance was the nudge I needed to get this book written. My gratitude for your friendship can never be measured. Can't wait to hit the road with you again, my friend!

I would like to thank my publisher and my editor for cutting my poetry lessons from my last book. Had they not cut them out, I would never have written this one. Enormous gratitude to my editor Kat Mototsune for not letting me settle for "choppy" and nudging me to dig deeper to find the thread. As always, this book is better because of you. Thank you to Mary Macchiusi, my publisher, for your patience. Writing a book during a pandemic sounds easy, but it wasn't, and I'm thankful for you gently nudging but never pushing. Can't wait to toast this book with you in real time, Aperol spritz in hand!

My two sisters, Janet and Alison, are the wisest, bravest women I know. Thank you for helping me keep my eye on the prize and cheering me on to the finish line. Weekly Zooms with you this past year were a blessing, as is having lived my whole life with both of you in it.

In my twenty-five plus teaching career, I have been blessed to be surrounded by some of the most dedicated educators you can imagine. Through their stead-fast belief in best practice and their continued desire to learn in order to teach, my work has grown to have meaning and purpose. You know who you are. Thank you.

There are many student samples in this book, and they represent only a fraction of the number of children I have had the pleasure of teaching over the years. As I always say, I am at my best when I have a book in my hand and a group of students around me. I am truly grateful for all my students have gifted me throughout my career, including these beautiful poems.

And finally, my three boys—Richard, Spencer, and Oliver. You see me at my worst and best, and love me through it all. You talked me through the rough patches of this book with love and patience, and never doubted I would finish. Whenever I talk with students about what the word *home* means, yours are the faces I see.

Professional Resources

Bernabei, Gretchen and Laura Van Prooyen (2020) *Text Structures from Poetry, Grades 4-12: Lessons to Help Students Read, Analyze, and Create Poems They Will Remember*. Los Angeles, CA: Corwin.

Booth, David and Bill Moore (2003) *Poems Please! Sharing Poetry with Children*. Markham, ON: Pembroke.

Cecil, Nancy Lee (1994) *For the Love of Language: Poetry for Every Learner*. Winnipeg, MB: Portage & Main.

Dorfman, Lynne R. and Rose Cappelli (2012) *Poetry Mentor Texts: Making Reading and Writing Connections, K-8*. Portland, ME: Stenhouse.

Fletcher, Ralph (2002) *Poetry Matters: Writing a Poem from the Inside Out*. New York, NY: HarperCollins.

Gear, Adrienne (2020) *Powerful Writing Structures*. Markham, ON: Pembroke.

Gear, Adrienne (2015) *Reading Power: Teaching Students to Think While They Read*. Markham, ON: Pembroke.

Heard, Georgia (1998) *Awakening the Heart: Exploring Poetry in Elementary and Middle School*. Portsmouth, NH: Heinemann.

Heard, Georgia (1989) *For the Good of the Earth and Sun: Teaching Poetry*. Portsmouth, NH: Heinemann.

Koch, Kenneth (1990) *Rose, Where Did You Get That Red? Teaching Great Poetry to Children*. New York, NY: Vintage Books.

Koch, Kenneth and Ron Padgett (1999) *Wishes, Lies, and Dreams: Teaching Children to Write Poetry*. New York, NY: Harper Perennial.

Lamott, Anne (1995) *Bird By Bird: Some Instructions on Writing and Life*. New York: NY: Anchor Books.

Latham, Irene and Charles Waters (2020) *Dictionary for a Better World: Poems, Quotes, and Anecdotes from A to Z*. Minneapolis, MN: Carolrhoda Books.

McPhillips, Shirley (2014) *Poem Central: Word Journeys with Readers and Writers*. Portland, ME: Stenhouse.

Padgett, Ron, editor (2000) *The Teachers & Writers Handbook of Poetic Forms*. New York, NY: Teachers & Writers Collaborative.

Parsons, Les (1992) *Poetry: Themes and Activities*. Markham, ON: Pembroke.

Protopropescu, Orel (2003) *Metaphors and Similes You Can Eat and 12 More Great Poetry Writing Lessons*. New York, NY: Scholastic.

Rosen, Michael (2019) *What Is Poetry? The Essential Guide to Reading & Writing Poems*. Somerville, MA: Candlewick Press.

Routman, Regie (2000) *Kid's Poems: Teaching First Graders to Love Writing Poetry*. New York, NY: Scholastic.

Rukeyser, Muriel. 1996. *The Life of Poetry*. Ashfield, MA: Paris Press.

Ruurs, Margriet (2013) *The Power of Poems*. Gainesville, FL: Maupin House.

VanDerwater, Amy Ludwig (2017) *Poems Are Teachers: How Studying Poetry Strengthens Writing in All Genres*. Portsmouth, NH: Heinemann.

https://suziebitner.com/poems/
https://poemanalysis.com/
https://clpe.org.uk/poetry
https://literarydevices.net/
https://www.poetry4kids.com/
https://www.familyfriendpoems.com/poems/
https://childrens-books.lovetoknow.com/
   Examples_of_Metaphor_Poems_for_Children
https://imaginationsoup.net/resources-teaching-writing-poetry-children/
https://www.poemsearcher.com/topic/repetitive

Index